Cambridge Elements

Elements in Greek and Roman Mythology
edited by
Roger D. Woodard
University of Buffalo

DIACHRONIC NARRATOLOGY IN GREEK MYTH

Silvio Bär
University of Oslo

Shaftesbury Road, Cambridge CB2 8EA, United Kingdom

One Liberty Plaza, 20th Floor, New York, NY 10006, USA

477 Williamstown Road, Port Melbourne, VIC 3207, Australia

314–321, 3rd Floor, Plot 3, Splendor Forum, Jasola District Centre, New Delhi – 110025, India

103 Penang Road, #05–06/07, Visioncrest Commercial, Singapore 238467

Cambridge University Press is part of Cambridge University Press & Assessment, a department of the University of Cambridge.

We share the University's mission to contribute to society through the pursuit of education, learning and research at the highest international levels of excellence.

www.cambridge.org
Information on this title: www.cambridge.org/9781009474986

DOI: 10.1017/9781009474993

© Silvio Bär 2025

This publication is in copyright. Subject to statutory exception and to the provisions of relevant collective licensing agreements, no reproduction of any part may take place without the written permission of Cambridge University Press & Assessment.

When citing this work, please include a reference to the DOI 10.1017/9781009474993

First published 2025

A catalogue record for this publication is available from the British Library

ISBN 978-1-009-47498-6 Hardback
ISBN 978-1-009-47503-7 Paperback
ISSN 2753-6440 (online)
ISSN 2753-6432 (print)

Cambridge University Press & Assessment has no responsibility for the persistence or accuracy of URLs for external or third-party internet websites referred to in this publication and does not guarantee that any content on such websites is, or will remain, accurate or appropriate.

For EU product safety concerns, contact us at Calle de José Abascal, 56, 1°, 28003 Madrid, Spain, or email eugpsr@cambridge.org

Diachronic Narratology in Greek Myth

Elements in Greek and Roman Mythology

DOI: 10.1017/9781009474993
First published online: November 2025

Silvio Bär
University of Oslo
Author for correspondence: Silvio Bär, silvio.baer@ifikk.uio.no

Abstract: *Diachronic Narratology in Greek Myth* looks at ancient Greek mythology from the viewpoint of its storytelling through time. There are hundreds of different figures and stories in Greek mythology, interconnected in a complex narrative network. While earlier research often sought to penetrate the core of the seemingly 'true' or 'original' myths, it is now better understood that the way the myths were conveyed constitutes their actual essence: how a story is told, and retold, cannot be separated from the story itself. Based on brief introductions to the basics of mythology and narratology, this Element offers a discussion of three paradigmatic characters from Greek mythology and their voyage through literary history: Odysseus, Herakles and Helen. It demonstrates how a narratological approach can enrich our perspective on, and understanding of, mythology.

Keywords: narratology, mythology, Odysseus, Herakles, Helen

© Silvio Bär 2025

ISBNs: 9781009474986 (HB), 9781009475037 (PB), 9781009474993 (OC)
ISSNs: 2753-6440 (online), 2753-6432 (print)

Contents

	Preliminary Remarks	1
1	Mapping the Territory: Myth and Diachronic Narratology	1
2	Case Study I: Odysseus	16
3	Case Study II: Herakles	25
4	Case Study III: Helen	36
5	Final Thoughts	45
	References	48

Preliminary Remarks

Abbreviations of ancient Greek and Roman authors and their works follow the conventions of *The Oxford Classical Dictionary* (*OCD*). Translations from Ancient Greek are mine unless otherwise noted. The spelling of mythical names follows the practice by Jenny March in *The Penguin Book of Classical Myths* (March 2009: 7): characters and places are by default spelt in their original Greek rather than their Latinized form (thus, e.g., 'Klytaimnestra', not 'Clytemnestra') unless the Latinized form is so established that the original Greek would appear obscure (thus, e.g., 'Oedipus', not 'Oidipus').

1 Mapping the Territory: Myth and Diachronic Narratology

1.1 What Is (a) Myth?

There are things in the world about which we seemingly know what they are, yet we are unable to define them adequately. Big universal ideas such as 'love', 'truth' and 'culture' are obvious such cases; and, at the time of writing – that is, about two years after the public launch of ChatGPT – concepts such as 'life', 'intelligence' and 'consciousness' also spring to mind. Admittedly, 'myth' and 'mythology' are perhaps not comparably burning topic of the day, but they nevertheless belong in the same category: for we all believe to know what a myth is – until we are asked to provide a precise definition of it. But how and why exactly do we know that the story of the Argonauts and their quest for the Golden Fleece is a myth, while the story of Snow White and the Seven Dwarfs or that of Perceval and his search for the Holy Grail are not? We cannot immerse ourselves into the intricacies of all the similarities and differences between myth, fairy tale and legend here; however, recognizing the notorious difficulty of defining 'myth', along with the necessity to juxtapose the genre with other – related, but different – genres and modes of narration, must at least be acknowledged.[1] Frustratingly, a look into the work of scholars of myth is of little help; on the contrary, the deeper one examines theories of myth, the more complex the picture becomes, because there is simply no scholarly consensus as to what a myth is.[2] And indeed, as early as 1974, the

---

[1] On the differences between myth and fairytale and/or legend, see e.g. Jolles (1930: 23–125); Dowden (1992: 6–7); Renger (2006: 70–105 *et passim*); Neumann (2013 *passim*); Zgoll (2019: 205–246). On definitions of 'myth' by comparison with other areas of study, see also Wellek & Warren (^{3}1970: 190): "'Myth'… points to, hovers over, an important area of meaning, shared by religion, folklore, anthropology, sociology, psychoanalysis, and the fine arts. In some of its habitual oppositions, it is contraposed to "history", or to "science", or to "philosophy", or to "allegory" or to "truth".'

[2] Gentile (2011) provides an insightful compilation of definitions, showing the wide variety of differing views. See further also, e.g., Honko (1972); Kirk (1973); Rogerson (1978–79); Dowden (1992: 3–7); Von Hendy (2001: 1–48); Csapo (2005: 1–9); Johnston (2018: 1–22).

British classicist Geoffrey S. Kirk stated that 'the nature of myth is still, in spite of the millions of printed words devoted to it, a confused topic' (Kirk 1974: 17) – an observation to which we can only add that another few millions of words on the topic have been printed in the meantime, only to reinforce and aggravate the problem identified by Kirk more than fifty years ago.

According to the *Greek-English Lexicon* by Henry George Liddell, Robert Scott and Sir Henry Stuart Jones (LSJ), the Ancient Greek noun *mŷthos* (μῦθος) has a wide range of meanings; it designates, inter alia, a 'tale', a 'story', a 'narrative' or simply 'fiction'. In other words, *mŷthos* encompasses anything that we would typically look for, and find, in the 'Fiction' section of a bookstore today. Already in antiquity, the Greek historians Herodotus (c. 484–425 BCE) and Thucydides (c. 460–400 BCE) used the term to denote an implausible tale without sufficient validity (Hdt. 2.35, 2.45.1; Thuc. 1.22.4) – a tale that may make a good story, but that cannot constitute the basis of historical investigation. And, along similar lines, the geographer Strabo (c. 64 BCE–c. CE 24) defined myths as 'things that are old, fabricated and marvellous', as opposed to history, which 'seeks the truth, no matter whether old or new' (*Geography* 11.5.3). So, even if modern scholarship does not agree on a clear-cut definition, we can agree that our understanding of myth is considerably narrower than this broad definition (otherwise, Snow White and Perceval would indeed fall into the same category). The *Oxford English Dictionary* (*OED*) defines 'myth' as 'a traditional story, typically involving supernatural beings or forces, which embodies and provides an explanation, aetiology or justification for something such as the early history of a society, a religious belief or ritual, or a natural phenomenon'.[3] Similarly, the American folklorist Alan Dundes, in the introduction to a collection of essays, defines myth even more succinctly, but aptly, as 'a sacred narrative explaining how the world and man came to be in their present form' (Dundes 1984b: 1). And indeed, almost all definitions, different as they may be in their details and their theoretical or ideological fundament, somehow relate myth to a 'time before time',[4] combined with one or the other form of explanatory function (called 'aetiology'), and involving divinities and/ or other human-like, supernatural beings.

The involvement of the divine sphere as a characteristic trait of myth undoubtedly indicates that there is an inherent relation between mythology and religion. This, in turn, begs the question as to how the two areas relate

---

[3] 'Mythology', in turn, is defined correspondingly as 'a body or collection of myths, esp[ecially] those relating to a particular person or thing, or belonging to a particular religious or cultural tradition'.

[4] On the close relation between mythology and historiography in antiquity, and the idea of myth as a form of 'early history', see e.g. Graf (1993 [1987]: 121–141).

to – and correlate with – each other. Clearly, one is not identical with the other, but one is not thinkable without the other either. The probably most memorable, and surely the most cited, explanation is that by the American historian of religion Joseph Campbell, who regards myth as 'other people's religion' and religion as 'misunderstood mythology', 'the misunderstanding consisting in the interpretation of mythic metaphors as references to hard fact' (Campbell 2002 [1986]: 27). And, whether we like it or not, Campbell does have a point; for indeed, I as a Christian (for example) would not be inclined to call the stories of the Old Testament 'myths', but at the same time I cannot deny the fact that (to pick a random example) the story of Moses' abandonment on the waters of the Nile strongly resembles, and in fact is structurally identical with, the myth of the abandonment of Romulus and Remus on the Tiber (or that of Oedipus in the woods). This understanding takes me to what I want to propose as my own definition of mythology: mythology is the narrative side of religion.[5] Religion, on the other hand, is mythology that is believed in and/or played out in performance. The performative side of religion is ritual; and ritual reconnected to myth raises a typical chicken-and-hen-problem – namely, what was first? The Dutch historian of religion Jan N. Bremmer summarizes the problem as follows:

> Although myths existed without rituals and rituals without myths, the two symbolic systems were often interrelated. This relationship is only gradually becoming clearer and is still the subject of lively debate. In the course of time, three possibilities have been suggested: ritual follows the pattern of myth; ritual generates myth; and ritual and myth arise at the same time, *pari passu.* (Bremmer 2021: 72–73)

A discussion of this complex debate and its long history would take us too far away from the focus of this introduction; suffice it to say that the ritual approach to the study of myth is not currently *à la mode* (and is not the focus of this Element either),[6] but nevertheless cannot go unmentioned in a discussion of questions relating to the definition of myth and mythology. What is crucial to be aware of, in any case, is, again, the aetiological aspect: the triangle 'religion – mythology – ritual' works only through the aetiological 'grease'.[7] Myths explain the world as it is on the basis of what happened in the past (within the system of mythology,

---

[5] The narrative nature of mythology is also at the heart of Northrop Frye's approach (Frye 1957: 131–239), according to whom all forms of literature and storytelling ultimately stem from myth, irrespective of the medium through which they are communicated (textually, orally, visually etc.).

[6] On the debate and its history, see e.g. Versnel (1993: 15–88); Von Hendy (2001: 77–112); Kowalzig (2007: 13–55); Bremmer (2010); Johnston (2018: 35–64); Bremmer (2021: 72–76); Edmunds (2021: 80–93).

[7] Contrast e.g. Johnston (2018: 58–64), who considers aetiology to be less important than generally considered, in my opinion playing down its importance too strongly.

references to an even earlier past – a mythical plupast – are not uncommon either, for example, when the heroes of Homer's *Iliad* talk about the good old days when their stronger and taller ancestors were still alive and active). Often, such explanations concern the presence and the functioning of an oracle, a cult, a festival and so on but also other things like, for example, natural phenomena and stellar constellations. An instructive and well-known example is the Eleusinian Mysteries, a cult of Demeter and Persephone at the Panhellenic Sanctuary of Eleusis near Athens, the origins of which are explained by the aetiological narration of Demeter's attempt to nurse and thus deify Demophon, the son of king Keleos of Eleusis, as recounted in the *Homeric Hymn to Demeter* (lines 231–255).[8] Some theoreticians of myth even go a step further and claim that mythic narration embedded in a ritualized setting had the potential to concretely influence and change the world view, at times even the actual behaviour, of its audience.[9] To summarize, we can say that through aetiology, myth and ritual acquire meaning and are concatenated with each other, and the present of a society and its views and values are thus connected to and explained by the past.

Finally, a word on scope: this Element is concerned with diachronic narratology in Greek myth – whereby 'Greek' refers to the culture of ancient Greece from the first written sources (i.e. Homer's epics the *Iliad* and the *Odyssey*, dated, very approximately, to c. 700 BCE) all the way through to what is commonly considered the nodal point between late antiquity and the early Byzantine era (which is – again, very approximately – set at c. CE 500; in terms of literary history, the gargantuan epic *Dionysiaca* by Nonnus of Panopolis often serves as a landmark). This Element does, however, not include the sphere of Roman mythology (nor the mythologies from any other culture, for that matter). Although Roman mythology was heavily influenced by Greek mythology, it has its decidedly own texture, its own twist. On the other hand, although the general considerations about the nature of mythology as delineated above are based on my reading and thinking about Greek mythology, I would nevertheless make a claim for a certain universal validity of them as far as the general outline is concerned – for the simple reason that the mentioned triangle 'religion – mythology – ritual' is of such a general nature that it seems difficult to imagine a culture that would not possess each of these aspects at least in its nucleus. Or, to put it in slightly different terms: as both religion and storytelling are universal to all human cultures, it must be concluded that the same applies to ritual practice and, above all, to mythology.[10]

---

[8] See e.g. Deichgräber (1950); Walton (1952); Richardson (1974: 231–242); Foley (1994: 65–75, 84–97).

[9] Claude Calame calls this the 'pragmatic effect' (see especially Calame 2009a [2000] and Calame 2011; Johnston 2015a: 14–16 for a critical discussion).

[10] On the evolutionary origins (and hence archetypal nature) of religion, see e.g. Boyer (2001).

1.2 What Is (Diachronic) Narratology?

Narratology is the systematic study and analysis of the mechanisms and parameters that constitute storytelling.[11] Since storytelling is an archetypal human activity, we can find narratives in all cultures, at all times and on all levels of complexity. Consequently, a narratological analysis can in principle be applied to any type of narrative, be it the bedtime stories parents tell their children or James Joyce's novel *Ulysses* (1922), with all its finicky intricacies. And, narratology is equally timeless, meaning that, for example, the Mesopotamian epic of Gilgamesh (dated to between c. 2100 and 1200 BCE) can be subject to a narratological study as much as the crime novels that are published here in Norway every year shortly before Easter ('Easter crime' being a uniquely Norwegian phenomenon).

In what follows, I provide a 'laundry list' of the most important parameters that are typically studied and analysed by narratologists, together with the most common terms that are used to describe the corresponding phenomena:

1) *Narrators and narratees*. Narratologists distinguish between the actual author of a text and the voice of the narrator that tells a story (in addition, sometimes the concept of the 'implied author' is added between the flesh-and-blood author and the narrator-figure of a text).[12] Another important distinction is that between the *homodiegetic narrator*, designating a narrator who is also a character in the story he/she tells, and the *heterodiegetic narrator*, who remains outside the story frame recounted.[13] Also of importance is the differentiation between the *primary narrator* (i.e. the narrator

---

[11] The following sketch is by no means meant to be an encyclopaedic introduction to the vast field of narratology; what follows are the basics that allow the reader to understand the fundament of this essay. There are several giants upon whose shoulders narratological theory of the twentieth century rests; see, inter alia and especially, Lämmert (1955); Hamburger (1973 [1968]); Chatman (1978); Genette (1980 [1972]); Booth (1983); Stanzel (1984 [1979]); Genette (1988 [1983]); Phelan & Rabinowitz (2005); Altman (2008); Fludernik (2009 [2006]); Bal (2017); Martínez & Scheffel (2019). For narratology in/and Classics, see especially Schmitz (2007 [2002]: 43–62); de Jong (2014a); de Jong (2019). For the terminology used, see the glossaries provided by de Jong (2001: xi–xix); Phelan & Rabinowitz (2005: 542–551); Fludernik (2009 [2006]: 150–162). See also the narratological dictionary by Prince (2003) and the online resource *The living handbook of narratology* (*LHN*).

[12] The concept of the implied author goes back to Booth (1983), but despite its usefulness (it helps us to talk about the author-figure without entering the realms of speculation about authorial intention), it is not universally accepted by narratologists. See e.g. Kindt & Müller (1999) and Heinen (2002) for discussions. An analogous concept is that of the implied reader: a hypothetical reader figure projected through the text (Iser 1974 [1972]).

[13] This comes close to, but is not fully congruent with, the distinction between first-person-narration and third-person-narration (on which see e.g. Stanzel 1984 [1979]: 80–88, 91–93 *et passim*). There is always an 'I' in a text, even if it does not participate in the events of the story, such as e.g. in Homer's *Iliad*, which clearly has a heterodiegetic narrator, but the 'I' still emerges from the narrator's call to the Muses at *Il.* 2.484–493.

sensu stricto, often described as 'auctorial' and/or 'omniscient') and the *secondary narrator* (i.e. a narratorial voice that is inserted into the main narrative, e.g. through the direct speech of a character telling a story in the story). On the other end, the *narratee* of a text is the hypothetical person to whom a story is told – who may, but need not, be identical with a text's actual reader (an obvious example to illustrate this point would be if someone secretly reads a letter that was in fact addressed to someone else).

2) *Focalization.* Focalization designates '[t]he perspective in terms of which the narrated situation and events are presented' (Prince 2003: 31); hence, the focalizer of a text is a figure (the narrator or a character in the story) through whose eyes the story is told and the events unfolding are seen. A common distinction is that between *external focalization* (i.e. an outside perspective on the text and its characters) and *internal focalization* (i.e. a from-within perspective, typically by a character of the story world). Further, one speaks of *embedded focalization* when the two levels are merged, be it when a character's viewpoint is embedded into the otherwise external focalization by the narrator, be it when narratorial ('auctorial') knowledge sneaks in to the speech of a character who thus knows more than he/she can in fact know.[14] In contrast, when the reader has more information than the character(s) in a text, one speaks of *dramatic irony.* Focalization can change in the course of a narrative.

3) *Narrative levels.* Narratologists distinguish between different types of narrative levels in relation to their fictional and/or ontological status. The *diegetic level* is the fictional frame of a story, the fictional world of all the characters and their fictional reality. The real world outside is correspondingly called the *extradiegetic level.* An extra narrative level embedded into the diegetic world is called the *intradiegetic level* (or *metadiegetic level*); consequently, a secondary narrator can also be called an intradiegetic (or metadiegetic) narrator. The diegetic and the extradiegetic levels are normally kept separate; when they are blended, a surprise effect arises – this is called a *metalepsis* or (somewhat more broadly) a *crossover* (a striking example would be the famous cameo appearances by Alfred Hitchcock in his films: a figure from the extradiegetic level intruding into the diegetic level).

4) *Time.* There are several important narrative aspects, and corresponding narratological concepts, related to time. First, there is the crucial distinction between *story time* and *narrating time*, the former relating to the time span covered by a given story, the latter to the actual time it takes to tell the story

---

[14] For further refinements of the concept of focalization, see e.g. Jahn (1999) and Nieragden (2002).

(a perspicuous example to illustrate this difference would be that of a play, the duration of which [= narrating time] may be about two hours, yet the play might cover events that span over several months or years in total [= story time]).[15] Secondly, and in close connection to the aforementioned point, there is also the question of narrative speed – the narration of an event can be extended (*extension*), compressed (*compression*), summarized (*summary*) or omitted entirely (*ellipsis*). Thirdly, the temporal order in which events are narrated also constitutes a crucial narrative parameter. The most basic order of narration is narration in chronological order (the default mode of storytelling children use: 'and then ... and then ... '). On the other hand, non-chronological storytelling (*anachrony*) also occurs; here an important distinction is that between *prolepsis* (foreshadowing: a pointing-forward to events ahead in time), *analepsis* (flashback/backshadowing: a pointing-backward to events that have already taken place) and *sideshadowing* (i.e. an allusion to an alternative version of a story or story detail that could have taken place, but did not happen). Finally, questions relating to when the narration of a story begins (*beginning*, *opening*) and when it ends (*ending*, *closure*) also belong to this category.

5) *Space*. Space as a narrative parameter is crucial for the simple reason that a fictional story world does not exist without a space within which the story unfolds and their characters can exist and act; 'all narratives imply a world with spatial extension, even when spatial information is withheld' (Ryan 2014: 796).[16] A narratological analysis of spatial parameters may for example look at how characters move in their space, how boundaries shape the narrative frame, how a change of location corresponds and/or contributes to the narrative development and how descriptions of spatial entities create a reality effect (*effet de réel*).[17] A term that is often used to denote the whereabouts of a scene in a story is *setting*. A literary topos that is intrinsically connected to space is that of the *locus amoenus*: an idealized, beautiful, paradise-like place; this topos is often combined with the practice of literary description (*ekphrasis*).

6) *Character.* The study of literary characters is a tricky matter because literary characters resemble – but in fact are not – flesh-and-blood people. However, in narratology, characters are understood as narrative entities as much as, for

---

[15] See Müller 1948.
[16] The study of space entered narratology relatively late, and its inclusion into the field is now commonly referred to as the 'spatial turn'. Important studies include Zoran (1984); Dennerlein (2009); Hallet & Neumann (2009); Warf & Arias (2009). On the spatial turn in cultural studies more broadly, see e.g. Weigel (2002).
[17] The concept of the *effet de réel* stems from Barthes (1968). An insightful discussion of the functions of space in ancient narrative is offered by Lowe (2000: 41–46).

example, narrators, time and space. Ideally, narratological character analysis understands literary characters as narrative constructs, but at the same time it takes into account the fact that 'literary narratives are structured in such a way as to create an illusion that they are reports about individuals' (Margolin 1995: 383), thus acknowledging both the constructedness of literary characters and their real-life resemblance.[18] Inter alia, narratologists analyse how fictional characters are constructed and developed (*characterization*) and how they speak (*character speech*). Characters travelling from one fictional frame to another (e.g. heroes from Homer's *Iliad* re-staged in Attic tragedy) are called *transtextual characters*; characters crossing over from one medium (e.g. text) to another (e.g. iconography) are called *transmedial characters*; characters at home in the worlds of different media are called *plurimedial characters*.[19]

7) *Minimal thematic units*.[20] Finally, minimal thematic units such as a specific narrative *pattern* or *motif* (called *leitmotif* when it occurs repeatedly and thus constitutes a red thread in a story) as well as literary commonplaces (*topoi* [singular *topos*]) are also subject to narratological analysis. At this point, the affinity of narratology to classical rhetoric, which traditionally analyses tropes (metaphors, metonymies, etc.) and figures of speech, becomes apparent, and there is a fine line between the two areas here.[21]

As will have become clear by now, narratologists tend to be more interested in the analysis of form than in the discussion of content.[22] However, this does not mean that narratology began as a purely formalistic discipline. We may just take a look at one of the founding documents of Western narrative, Homer's *Odyssey*, to see how strongly connected narrative phenomena and a broader literary interpretation can be.[23] For example, any reader of the *Odyssey* will notice that the epic has a conspicuously reticent, non-intrusive (in narratological jargon: covert) heterodiegetic primary narrator in Books 1–8 and 13–24,

---

[18] Important contributions to narratological character analysis are, inter alia, those by Jannidis (2004) and Frow (2014). See further Bal (2017: 105–108) on why characters are not intuitively understood as narrative entities.

[19] On transtextuality, see Richardson (2010); Philipowski (2019); Bär (2024b); Bär (2025); on transmediality, Thon (2016); on plurimediality, Johnston (2018: 156–163 *et passim*, with 309n.12 for further references).

[20] The term is borrowed from Prince (2003: 55).

[21] Indeed, the term 'topos' comes from rhetorical theory; see Curtius (1953 [1948]: 79–105).

[22] Historically, narratology is a child of structuralism (which, in turn, stems from Russian formalism, the first school of literary theory that exclusively looked at form instead of content). Stevens (2015: 135–159) offers an overview of the formalist approaches in literary theory since the early twentieth century.

[23] Comprehensive narratological analyses of the *Odyssey* are offered e.g. by Richardson (1990 *passim*); Latacz (1996 [1989]: 135–155); Louden (1999); Lowe (2000: 129–156); Saïd (2011 [1998]: 95–222); Cook (2014). Further, see also de Jong's (2001) narratological commentary.

whereas Books 9–12 (the well-known *Apologoi*) are reported by Odysseus personally in first-person narration – that is, by a homodiegetic secondary narrator – in an extended analepsis (Odysseus' narratees are the Phaiakians on the isle of Scheria, while we as readers are, in a manner of speaking, eavesdropping). This change of narrative voice and narrative level does not only constitute one of the most influential models for Western narrative, it also raises the question of Odysseus' credibility as an intradiegetic narrator: Can Odysseus, the prototypical liar and trickster, really be trusted when he recounts all his fairy-tale-like adventures? And what does that tell us about the role and the character of the hero more generally? Odysseus is thus the first example of yet another type of narrator, the so-called 'unreliable narrator'; and a narratological analysis of the voices in the *Odyssey* is undoubtedly the key to fleshing out the vexed question of fiction vs truth – a question that lies at the very heart of this epic.[24]

Moreover, as is well known, the *Odyssey* does not start at the beginning of Odysseus' voyage, but towards its end, at a divine council on Mount Olympus: Athene takes advantage of Poseidon's absence so that she can convince Zeus that he should finally release Odysseus from the isle of Ogygia, where the immortal nymph Kalypso has been holding him prisoner for as many as seven years (*Od.* 1.1–95). This late beginning, in combination with the subsequent shift from a heterodiegetic to a homodiegetic narrator, does not only lend variety to the narrative, it also enables the author to omit the least eventful, but longest (and thus dullest), part of Odysseus' absence from home: his sojourn on the isle of Ogygia, probably characterized by a lot of boredom. Thus, the major part of the epic's story time is actually a huge ellipsis. In terms of setting, then, we can notice that the beginning on Mount Olympus stands in contrast to where the rest of the *Odyssey* mostly takes place, namely on the sea and on islands (but rarely on the mainland), and that the change of location and especially the crossing of boundaries often mark some sort of rite of passage, which thus prepares for Odysseus' final homecoming (whereby Odysseus, ironically enough, does not recognize his home when he finally arrives on Ithaca [*Od.* 13.187–218]).

Another point that a narratologically minded reader will notice are the repeated allusions to king Agamemnon's fate – his homecoming and how he was killed by his wife Klytaimnestra and her lover Aigisthos upon arrival – that are interspersed across the *Odyssey*. Narratologically, these are analepses to an event that took place a few years before the time frame of the *Odyssey*, while for us as readers, they constitute glances at what we may perceive as 'alternative

---

[24] The concept of the unreliable narrator stems from Booth (1983). On the question of whether the *Apologoi* may be considered a 'lie', see § 2 below.

reality'. Through these analepses, Odysseus' homecoming – about which there can, in fact, be no doubt as it is part of the overarching mythical story frame – is constantly put into question. On the one hand, there is dramatic irony at work insofar as we, the readers, know of Odysseus' eventual homecoming, whereas he, as an innerfictional character, does not; on the other, the security of our knowledge is constantly undermined by those analepses that offer us a glimpse at the death of one of Odysseus' combatants by the hand of his wife, and we may thus wonder whether Odysseus might, after all, encounter a similar fate.[25]

While there can be no doubt that narratology is far from being formalistic, it had, for a long while, a blind spot when it comes to the challenges presented by different genres and corresponding generic differences, conventions and expectations because the first narratologists were mostly modernists who developed their theories and methods on the basis of novels from the nineteenth and twentieth century. Another point is that for an equally long time, narratology was almost exclusively synchronous, that is, narratologists would typically not analyse texts from different periods and compare their narrative peculiarities with each other, but they would mostly focus on one specific text and/or author (or a series of texts from approximately the same genre and the same period at the most) – a phenomenon that has recently been described as 'narratology's "presentist" bias' (Birke, von Contzen & Kukkonen 2022: 28). It is only after the turn of the millennium that narratology gradually opened up to the comparative study of narrative phenomena in ancient as well as mediaeval literature.[26] In an important position paper from 2014, the Dutch

---

[25] See the study by Olson (1990) on the narrative function of these analepses (with 57n.1 for references to earlier discussions). See also Alden (2017: 77–100), and Schmitz (1994) on further narrative techniques that undermine the reader's security concerning Odysseus' homecoming.

[26] In 2003, Monika Fludernik made a call for a cross-disciplinary 'diachronization of narratology' (Fludernik 2003). This call was answered and adapted to the needs of ancient narrative by Irene de Jong (de Jong 2014b), and along similar lines, Eva von Contzen has advocated for the introduction of diachronic narratology into the study of mediaeval literature (von Contzen 2014; von Contzen 2018). Consequently, in 2018, Fludernik spoke of the ongoing 'diachronic turn in narratology that is slowly making headway' (Fludernik 2018: 330). Indeed, between 2004 and 2021, five volumes of the *Studies in Ancient Greek Narrative* series were published, constituting, in its entirety, an overview of the major narrative parameters of Greek narrative (narrators and narratees: de Jong, Nünlist & Bowie 2004; time: de Jong & Nünlist 2007; space: de Jong 2012; characterization: De Temmerman & van Emde Boas 2017; speech: de Bakker & de Jong 2021). Further, see also the *Handbuch Historische Narratologie*, covering ancient, mediaeval and early-modern narrative (von Contzen & Tilg 2019), and the *Handbook of Diachronic Narratology*, studying narrative parameters in European literatures ranging from antiquity to the present (Hühn, Pier & Schmid 2023). On the important distinction between historical and diachronic narratology, see Birke, von Contzen & Kukkonen (2022: 30): 'The diachronic approach ... includes texts from different periods and aims to trace developments across these periods, while the historical approach foregrounds a corpus of texts from a single historical period.'

classicist and narratologist Irene de Jong identified the main tasks of diachronic narratology in Classics as follows:

> What is the history of the first-person novel, of narratorial comments, of audience-address, of the *locus amoenus*, etc.? Some narrative devices have long been identified and studied ..., but narratology has brought together, systematised, and much expanded the number of narrative devices found employed by authors in narrative texts, and thereby opened the way to the study of their use over time ... One of the central research questions of diachronic narratology is that of the relationship between form and function: how does one and the same device acquire ever new functions, depending on the exigencies of a genre, the predilections of an author, the theme of the narrative, or the taste of an age? (de Jong 2014b: 115, 118)

In summary, we can state that narratology is an established field of studies that has undergone considerable development in the past two decades and that is still in a state of change. In what follows, I identify and reflect upon some challenges we encounter when we apply narratological questions and methods to the study of mythical narratives.

1.3 Diachronic Narratology Applied to the Study of Myth

Despite the 'presentist bias' by which it was affected for several decades, narratology has, in fact, its roots in the study of myth and folktale. First, there was the forefather of narratology, the Soviet folklorist Vladimir Propp, who, under the influence of Russian formalism, developed a formalist approach to analysing Russian folktales in his study *Morphology of the Folktale* (published in Russian in 1928; first translated into English in 1958; second revised English edition from 1968). Propp's theory revolves around identifying recurring narrative elements and character types in folktales, suggesting that these elements follow a predictable pattern of functions. He thus identifies a total of thirty-one functional patterns, such as, for example, 'the hero's departure', 'the hero's victory' and 'the hero's return'. Furthermore, Propp also identifies seven character types that appear and reappear in all these tales; these characters perform specific functions within the narrative structure of a tale. Secondly, in critical dialogue with Propp, the French anthropologist and ethnologist Claude Lévi-Strauss also proposed a theory of myth that looks at underlying structures and patterns, but with a stronger emphasis on the 'paradigmatic' instead of the 'syntagmatic' level. Central to Lévi-Strauss' theory of myth is the concept of the 'mytheme', denoting the smallest meaningful unit of mythic structure in analogy to phonemes and morphemes in language. Lévi-Strauss thus argues that all myths from all cultures are composed of a finite set of mythemes arranged in various combinations and permutations.[27]

Irrespective of all their merits and influence, Propp's and Lévi-Strauss' theories suffer from several major flaws. One of them is that their claim for universal validity makes them attackable; another is that they are what I previously said narratology was not (or not meant to be) – namely, too formalistic. However, it is important to acknowledge that the origins of narratology stem from those structural(ist) studies in mythology. My own approach is neither devoted to a specific theory nor is it purely formalistic – but it feeds on formal(istic) approaches occasionally, and the discussion of recurring patterns and motifs is crucial in many instances. Furthermore, the application of narratological methods to the study of myth entails a few further caveats, which I need to address in what follows.

One major issue is this: myth is narrative – but myth is not a genre. Rather, myths constitute the basis of numerous literary genres for which they provide the 'raw material', with which people in antiquity were already familiar. However, the myths *are* not those genres. To be concrete, mythology provides the backbone of religious (or religiously motivated) genres such as hymns, cult songs and prayers; it forms the basis of practically all of epic and tragedy,[28] and it is also entrenched in many other genres such as comedy, lyric, epinician, historiography, the novel, etc. It would probably be difficult to find an ancient literary genre that has no relationship with mythology whatsoever. Consequently, any discussion of mythology in a diachronic perspective must necessarily incorporate a discussion of the genres to which one or the other myth is connected; studying diachronic mythology means automatically also looking at the development and crossing of genres and thus, ultimately, at the history of literature as such. In this context, it is also paramount to avoid what I call the 'urmyth fallacy': in the 1890s, the then influential British social anthropologist and folklorist James G. Frazer claimed that different versions of a similarly or identically structured mythical narrative should be regarded as 'corrupted' developments of an older, 'purer' original myth – an urmyth of primordial origin, created by some sort of natural genius.[29] Today, this view is

---

[27] Propp's theories are concentrated in the monograph mentioned (Propp 1968 [1928]), whereas those of Lévi-Strauss are interspersed across his life work (see especially Lévi-Strauss 1955 and Lévi-Strauss 1963 [1958]). For a comparison between the two, see Shishkoff (1976) and Dundes (1997). Further, see also Deliège (2004 [2001]: 95–107); Csapo (2005: 190–199 *et passim*); Doniger (2009); Zgoll (2019: 97–108); Edmunds (2021: 125–141).

[28] Of the thirty-one Attic tragedies that have been fully preserved, only Aeschylus' *The Persians* (premiered in 472 BCE) is not based on myth.

[29] Frazer was the main representative of a group of scholars known as the 'Cambridge Ritualists'. His *opus magnum* was his study *The Golden Bough*, in which he situated the theory of the urmyth within the context of a comparative reconstruction of ancient religious history. For the complex

rightly considered outdated – yet it often proves to be still influential through the backdoor, not least via the more formalist approaches. Rather, myth and genre are intimately connected with each other; hence, instead of attempting to 'unveil' the purportedly 'authentic' myths that underlie the genres through which they are communicated, the task of a narratologist analysing mythology in a diachronic perspective is to pay attention to the reciprocity between myth and genre. Or, to quote the American classicist and historian of religion Sarah Iles Johnston, 'rather than bemoaning the fact that the Greeks' ideas about the gods and heroes come to us mostly through fictionalizing art and literature, we should acknowledge that those portraits, cumulatively, *were* the gods and heroes', and '[w]hen characters are presented through more than one narrative ..., each narrative offers a different instantiation of that character from the others' (Johnston 2018: 156).[30] To this (correct and important) observation, I would only add that similar differences in instantiation equally apply to many other narrative parameters aside from character, as will be demonstrated in the subsequent case studies that take their starting point from mythical characters, but look at various other narrative aspects from a diachronic angle, too (§ 2–4).

Another point, closely linked to the aforementioned issue and important to bear in mind, is the fact that because of the traditionality of mythology, the principal mythical story frames were usually already known to the audience – a fact of which the ancients were patently aware, as a fragment by the comic poet Antiphanes (c. 404–334 BCE) demonstrates, stating that 'tragedy is a blessed / genre in all respects, as the stories are from the beginning / recognized by the spectators / before anyone even says a word' (fr. 189.1–4 *PCG*). To re-use the *Odyssey* example from above (§ 1.2), Homer's audience (as well as later, post-Homeric recipients) knew that Odysseus was eventually going to return home. Similarly, Oedipus always kills his father and marries his mother, Jason always captures the Golden Fleece, Orpheus always fails in his attempt to retrieve Eurydice from the Underworld, etc. As a result of this, from a reader-response perspective suspense is of a completely different nature as compared to how we typically think of it. To our understanding, suspense is typically seen as a 'state of uncertainty, anticipation and curiosity as to the outcome of a story

---

genesis and reception history of the study, published in various editions and versions, see Fraser (1990). Further, see also Csapo (2005: 57–67); Johnston (2018: 35–40); Zgoll (2019: 135–143).

[30] Apart from Johnston's (2018) excellent study, see also Johnston (2015a) and Johnston (2015b). The idea of myth as poetry was already proposed by Howald (1937). I disagree with Zgoll (2019: 41), who speaks of 'the literary fallacy of myth research' ('die literarische Falle der Mythosforschung') and argues for giving preference to 'the study of simple and aesthetically unassuming representations of the material' ('Untersuchung schlichter und künstlerisch weitgehend anspruchsloser Stoffdarstellungen'), referring to sources such as Apollodorus' *Library*.

or play, or any kind of narrative' (Cuddon 1991 s.v.). In contrast, suspense in *mŷthos*-based genres was primarily nourished by the dramatic irony that arose from the audience's superior knowledge, heightened by a tension resulting from the inability to communicate this superior knowledge to the characters who are constrained to their innerfictional reality (i.e. the inability to metaleptically transcend the barrier between the extradiegetic and the diegetic level),[31] further coupled with the question of *how* exactly the expected outcome of a story was going to occur. Alternatively, spectators and/or readers may also sometimes have engaged in what Johnston (2015a: 204) terms 'willful forgetfulness', that is, the temporary suppression or suspension of one's previous knowledge about the outcome of a story in order to enjoy it afresh (a mechanism that also enables activities such as the repeated consumption of a favourite episode from a TV series *vel sim.*). In addition, an author could also heighten the suspense by sowing doubt in the reader's expectations – like in the *Odyssey* example discussed above (§ 1.2), by interspersing the narrative with allusions to the fate of another hero who was not welcomed warmly, but killed deviously, by his wife. Thus, a cognitive dissonance arises between what the recipient knows must and will happen and what the text suggests may perhaps happen differently, or not at all.[32]

The fact that an ancient author would primarily need to work on the 'how' of his presentation of a myth, along with a general tendency of classical mythology towards being a permeable system open to variants and variations, leads to yet another consequence: we as readers and interpreters of ancient myths have to constantly deal with the question of how we should evaluate a variation, a change or an innovation in a mythical tale – whether, as it were, we should attribute it to the world of mythology or to the world of genre, or a combination of the two. That said, we must not fall into the trap of wanting to search for an 'urmyth', as emphasized above; on the other hand, ignoring the wide range of variants and variations by simply describing them as characteristically inherent to mythology without any further differentiation would be far too simplistic. This, in turn, also leads to questions about the canonical value of certain texts, certain genres and/or certain versions of a myth. An example that may illustrate this point comes from the probably most influential drama of all times: *Oedipus the King* by Sophocles (c. 497/6–406/5 BCE), first performed in Athens in c. 429 BCE. The gory climax of this tragedy is the moment when a messenger reports on what happened after Oedipus uncovered the horrible truth about his

---

[31] On this effect, see e.g. Chatman (1978: 59–60).
[32] On suspense in ancient Greek literature, see the volume by Konstantakos & Liotsakis (2021), with the contribution by Scodel (2021) discussing suspense in the Homeric epics. See further Baroni (2007: 269–295) on forms of suspense that are not contingent upon an unknown outcome.

past, that is, that he had unwittingly killed his father Laios and married his mother Jocasta: Jocasta has taken her own life (lines 1234–1267), and Oedipus has blinded himself in anguish (lines 1268–1279). The motif of Oedipus' self-blinding is so well known that we can hardly imagine the ending of the story to be any different. However, according to several parallel sources, there is in fact considerable variation.[33] A reference in the *Odyssey* indicates that after his discovery, Oedipus, distressed though he was, continued to govern Thebes (*Od.* 11.271–280), and the *Iliad* mentions that he later fell in battle and was honoured with funeral games (*Il.* 23.678–680).[34] This demonstrates that Homer followed a tradition in which the blinding did not take place (for a blind man cannot fight in battle), and the allusive character of the references suggests that this tradition must have been widely known (otherwise, the audience would not have understood the allusions). The motif of Oedipus' blinding, on the other hand, can be found in many sources, yet there is variation as to who inflicts it: one tradition says that Oedipus curses himself and is thus struck by blindness (schol. Eur. *Phoen.* 61), another that his foster father Polybos blinds him (schol. Eur. *Phoen.* 26), another that Laios' servants 'destroy his pupils' (Eur. *Oed.* fr. 541 *TrGF*). Furthermore, iconographic evidence attests to yet another version, namely that of Oedipus being blinded by order of Kreon.[35] It is noteworthy that in none of these traditions, Oedipus inflicts the blinding on himself by his own hands, and it could therefore be tempting to assume that Sophocles might have invented the self-blinding for dramaturgic reasons. However, this hypothesis is contradicted by a mention of the self-blinding in Aeschylus' *Seven against Thebes* (lines 772–784), a play that precedes Sophocles' *Oedipus the King* by several decades (it was produced in 467 BCE).

At the end of the day, we are left with a riddle. Sophocles' tragedy is the only Oedipus drama that has survived, and following the positive verdicts by literary critics (beginning with Aristotle), it is not coincidental that this and not any other such drama has stood the test of time. However, this does not change the fact that our perspective is biased, as it is solely focused through the lens of Sophocles. The question therefore arises as to how we should evaluate all the variants. Are they all just variations within a wide spectrum of mythical possibilities? Or is the blinding motif a specifically tragic trait, the concrete implementation of which

---

[33] See Edmunds (1985: 13–17); Gantz (1993: 492–502); Edmunds (2006: 11–54 *passim*); Laes (2024: 23–24). An overview of all relevant Greek texts that deal with the Oedipus myth is provided by Edmunds (2006: 32–33). On the motif of blinding and blindness in Sophocles, see also Buxton (1980).

[34] On Oedipus' death in epic, which deviates considerably from the version known from Sophocles' tragedy *Oedipus at Colonus*, see de Kock (1961: 8–20) and Cingano (1992).

[35] On three Etruscan urns, two soldiers are shown holding Oedipus, and a third one executes the blinding, while Kreon stands by, watching. See Krauskopf (1974: 52–53) and Edmunds (1985: 16).

varies from tragedy to tragedy, whereas the complete absence of the motif (along with the idea that Oedipus continues his life as a king after his discovery) is perhaps characteristic of the epic tradition? And how did the fact that so many variants existed affect the suspense factor for Sophocles' contemporary audience, the degree of the dramatic irony involved and the surprise (or shock) effect when the messenger reported on what happened? I do not have answers to these questions – but we must bear in mind that such questions continue to emerge when we study mythology in a diachronic perspective.

In what follows, I offer a discussion of three of the most colourful characters from Greek mythology and their voyage through literary history: Odysseus, Herakles and Helen. By looking at the diachronic development of these three characters, I intend to demonstrate how a narratological approach can enrich our perspective on, and understanding of, mythology in general. I have chosen these three characters because they are still widely known today and because they can be regarded as paradigmatic when it comes to their uninterrupted cultural significance from antiquity to the present. In line with the necessity to pay attention to the reciprocity between myth and genre, as outlined above, my focus will mainly be on the representation of these figures in literary texts from different genres and periods, yet the picture will be broadened by occasional side glances at wider cultural aspects such as visual material here and there.

2 Case Study I: Odysseus

2.1 The Homeric Odysseus: Rhetorical Failures and Lies

Since we have used the *Odyssey* as an example to illustrate what a narratological analysis can accomplish (§ 1.2), it seems appropriate that we spend a little time with that epic's protagonist, Odysseus. As noted previously, Odysseus is not only a mythical figure whose stories are narrated but he is also a prominent narrator himself, as the Homeric *Apologoi* (*Odyssey* Books 9–12) make abundantly clear. However, his career as a 'man of words' begins already in the *Iliad*, where he is a central figure too (although not a protagonist).[36] Aside from being a warrior (see especially his aristeia at *Il.* 11.396–486), he is already in the *Iliad* renowned for his superior intelligence (he is repeatedly called 'equivalent to Zeus in terms of wisdom' [*Il.* 2.169, 2.407, 2.636, 10.137] by the primary narrator) and his rhetorical skills. In this capacity, he is chosen, together with Phoinix and the Greater Ajax, to take the lead in the embassy that is sent to

---

[36] On Odysseus in the *Iliad*, see Coleman-Norton (1927); Stanford (1963: 11–19 *et passim*); Folzenlogen (1965); Cramer (1973); Pucci (1987: 143–147 *et passim*); Cairns (2015); Nightingale (2016: 122–130).

Achilles in order to convince him to relinquish his anger and to rejoin the battle (*Il.* 9.162–657). Odysseus speaks first (lines 225–306), reminding Achilles of the dire consequences of his abstention from fighting and his obligation to help; his speech is followed by that of Phoinix, who strikes a paternal tone (lines 434–605), whereas Ajax' speech is rather short and brusque (lines 624–642), in line with this warrior's uncouth nature.[37] From a rhetorical point of view, Odysseus' speech almost constitutes a schoolbook example of a carefully arranged piece of rhetoric – indeed, Odysseus' style of speech (his character speech) was repeatedly classified as a model of the grand style of rhetoric (*genus grande*) by ancient critics.[38] However, despite the sophistication of his speech, Odysseus is unsuccessful with his rhetoric, for Achilles replies bitterly that he will neither rejoin the battle nor accept Agamemnon's gifts as long as the latter has not adequately atoned for his insult (lines 308–429). Thus, the first attempt at rhetorical persuasion in Western civilization is a failure; '[i]n the first work of European literature we are brought face to face with some of the limitations of rhetoric' (Kennedy 1999: 12). Even more serious, though, is perhaps the fact that Odysseus' career as the prototypical man of words starts with such an immense setback. For the sake of the narrative, however, Odysseus' failure proves to be crucial, for had he been successful in convincing Achilles to re-enter the fray, the further narrative development would not have enfolded as it does. A rhetorically successful Odysseus would have led to a completely different *Iliad*, or no *Iliad* whatsoever.[39]

Turning to the *Odyssey*, we can find an Odysseus figure who is considerably more successful with his rhetoric. However, he has to learn a hard lesson first because he makes a serious mistake in the initial stages of his voyage: as he reports at the beginning of the *Apologoi* (*Odyssey* Book 9), Odysseus and his comrades are trapped in the cave of the Cyclops Polyphemos, the one-eyed giant and cannibal, and they are only able to escape thanks to Odysseus' famous trick (i.e. they intoxicate and blind the Cyclops with a wooden stake, and then they manage to leave the cave by clinging to the bellies of the giant's sheep), and since Odysseus has previously introduced himself as 'Nobody' (*Oûtis* [Οὖτις], a folk-etymological pun on his real name), Polyphemos is unsuccessful in persuading his comrades to come to his aid when he is in pain. However, when Odysseus is already back on his ship and feels safe, he taunts Polyphemos by revealing his true identity (lines 502–505). Consequently,

---

[37] Analyses of the three speeches are provided by Lohmann (1970: 213–282); Walsh (2005: 187–204); Kennedy (1999: 8–12); Dularidze (2005). Further, see also Beck (2005a: 199–202).

[38] See Russell (1981: 137–139).

[39] See also Montanari (2017), who conjectures that the embassy in *Iliad* 9 may have been an invention by Homer, not traditionally anchored in the Trojan Saga.

Polyphemos prays to his father Poseidon for revenge (lines 528–535), begging him to make Odysseus suffer as much as possible on his voyage, 'that he may come home late and miserably, losing all his comrades, / on a foreign ship, and that he may find sorrows in his house' (lines 534–535). It is thus Odysseus' lack of self-containment, his *hýbris* (ὕβρις, 'overconfidence', 'complacency'),[40] that makes him impulsively succumb to his urge to mock the Cyclops, who as a result provokes the hero's prolonged and painful return voyage, his proverbial *nóstos* (νόστος, 'return home'). There are several more prolepses to the circumstances of Odysseus' return in the *Odyssey*,[41] but this one is special insofar as it is not only a foreshadowing, but in fact the cause of Odysseus' long and miserable trip. In rhetorical terms, Odysseus misjudges the *kairós* (καιρός), the 'right moment'. Focke (1943: 159–160) notes the grandiose style of Polyphemos' prayer, which stands in contrast to his otherwise uncultivated nature. Odysseus and Polyphemos appear to have exchanged roles: while Odysseus, at a moment when he should have remained silent, speaks out, Polyphemos, in his prayer to his father, reaches unforeseen rhetorical heights. In narratological terms, Odysseus' inappropriate use of words results in the extreme narrative extension of the *Odyssey*; while the *Iliad* would not exist without Odysseus' rhetorical failure, the *Odyssey* would not exist without Odysseus' supercilious behaviour, his absence of self-control and his verbal excess towards Polyphemos.[42]

From this moment, Odysseus is extremely careful about disclosing his identity. He does reveal it to the Phaiakians by officially introducing himself to Alkinoos (*Od.* 9.19–20) before he begins to tell all his adventures, but only after having concealed who he really is for several days. Thereafter, he (indirectly) reconfirms his identity by reporting the incident with Polyphemos; shouting 'Odysseus, the destroyer of cities, has blinded you' (*Od.* 9.504) has a metaleptic quality, as the exclamation reaches its audience on the metadiegetic, the diegetic and the extradiegetic level. Simultaneously, a tension arises between Odysseus' lack of concern in the past and his extreme diligence now; by telling his narratees about his previous carelessness regarding his identity, he simultaneously shows them (and us) that he has fundamentally changed his behaviour in this respect.

This takes us to the question of Odysseus as a liar. As briefly discussed previously already (§ 1.2), we may justifiably wonder whether Odysseus can be

---

[40] On Odysseus' *hýbris*, see Friedrich (1991).
[41] *Od.* 2.174–176, 11.113–117, 13.131–132 and 15.176–177; see de Jong (2001: 55). On the *nóstos* theme in ancient Greek epic, see Frame (1978).
[42] In a manner of speaking, we are implicitly confronted with a form of sideshadowing (a common Homeric technique; see Nesselrath 1992: 5–38), as we are allowed a glimpse at an alternative fictional reality in which the work of fiction is not realized or at least considerably truncated.

trusted about the truth of his *Apologoi*. In narratological terms, the question is whether Odysseus should be regarded as an unreliable narrator, and if so, how far his (lack of) reliability goes and what the implication of this is for the overall understanding of his character. It is noteworthy that Odysseus concocts several cock-and-bull-stories in the second half of the *Odyssey*, when he has already arrived on Ithaca, but still remains in disguise so as not to expose himself in a situation where he is not sure about whom he can trust (as the suitors of his wife Penelope are battening on his estate and present a life-threatening danger for him). On three occasions, he tells elaborate lies about his identity and his provenance: first to Athene, whom he does not recognize because she has transformed herself into a young shepherd (*Od.* 13.256–286), then to his loyal swineherd Eumaios (*Od.* 14.191–359) and finally to none other than his own wife (*Od.* 19.165–342). Each time, he varies the details of his lies, but their quintessence always remains the same: he claims to be an uprooted veteran of the Trojan War, originating from the isle of Crete and in kinship with the Cretan king Idomeneus (who indeed was a participant in the Trojan War according to the *Iliad*). A detailed analysis and discussion of these highly intricate (and equally ironic) 'Cretan lies' cannot be offered here.[43] What is relevant for our purposes is that Odysseus, despite his clearly fraudulent intent, maintains a nucleus of truth by making his deceptive *alter ego* a distorted version of himself, that is, a displaced homecomer from the Trojan War on an adventurous return voyage. The Cretan lies are, overall, lies indeed, yet there is also a spark of truth in them. This, in turn, gives rise to the assumption that also the *Apologoi* may partly be true, partly contrived.

It is important to note that the *Apologoi* are narrated *before* the Cretan lies, meaning that a reader who initially takes the former at face value may in retrospect have second thoughts about their truthfulness in light of the deceptive character of the latter. At this point, we must remember that the major mythical figures and their principal story frames were typically already known to the audience,[44] and therefore, a contemporary audience would at least have had an approximate idea as to where to place a tale on the 'spectrum of truthfulness'. However, we saw before that the repeated analepses to king Agamemnon's death by the hand of his wife sow doubt onto the expected positive outcome of Odysseus' homecoming despite all the traditionality of the tale (§ 1.2); likewise, here too doubt is sown *ex posteriori* onto the validity of Odysseus' *Apologoi*. In

---

[43] For analyses of the Cretan lies, see Stanford (1950); Trahman (1952); Walcot (1977); Haft (1984); Reece (1994); Clayton (2004: 53–82); Maronitis (2004: 147–163); Tsanava (2009); Alden (2017: 263–303 *passim*).

[44] On the traditionality of the Odysseus figure, see e.g. Philippson (1947); on the traditionality of the *Apologoi*, Burgess (2017).

my opinion, the point is not so much to find an unequivocal answer to the question of whether or not Odysseus is a liar but, rather, to acknowledge the partial unreliability of his role as a secondary narrator as perceived by the readers of the *Odyssey*.[45] As a matter of fact, there are several 'authentification devices' spread across the main story (i.e. the heterodiegetic narrative in Books 1–8 and 13–24), both in the mouth of the primary narrator and several secondary narrators, that refer to details reported in the *Apologoi* and thus add credibility to Odysseus' homodiegetic narrative.[46] For example, in Book 8, a knot is mentioned that the sorceress Circe (whose story Odysseus narrates in Book 10) once taught Odysseus (lines 447–448). The narration of such a detail outside the *Apologoi* does, however, not automatically authenticate their *entire* truthfulness; it only attests to the fact that there is, as it were, a minimum of truth in Odysseus' narration – yet there is also a minimum of truth in the Cretan lies. Furthermore, the fact that Odysseus does not mention the knot in his own narration of the events in Book 10 may not only be seen as a narrative ellipsis, it may also be taken as an indication that Odysseus' account does indeed not constitute the full truth.

The function of the *Apologoi* in relation to the *Odyssey*'s main narrative has previously been discussed in scholarship, as has the understanding of Odysseus as a poetic *alter ego* of the Homeric narrator, and there is neither room nor need to further engage in this discussion here.[47] What is important to keep in mind for our purposes is Odysseus' ambiguity in his role as a narrator – an ambiguity that is created by the hero's narration oscillating between reliability and unreliability, the mode of narration being tightly connected to Odysseus' position as a partly reliable, partly unreliable narrator figure.

2.2 The Post-Homeric Odysseus: Rhetorical Success – and More Lies

Dante Alighieri (c. 1265–1321), the father of Italian poetry and the Italian language, has his own fictionalized self guided by the (equally fictionalized) Roman poet Vergil through the *Inferno* ('Hell'), the inspection and description

---

[45] See e.g. Parry (1994); Richardson (1996); de Jong (2001: 212, 221–222). Parry (1994: 17) may be right that 'Odysseus would have much to lose quite needlessly by lying to the [Phaiakians]' and that the *Apologoi* are thus 'by no means fabrications', but this does not efface, from a reader-response perspective, the retroactive doubts that one experiences after having been confronted with the Cretan lies.

[46] See de Jong (2001: 221–222).

[47] See e.g. Suerbaum (1968); Most (1989); Maronitis (2004: 101–115). Further references at Pratt (1993: 2n.1) and Rabel (1999: 181n.39–40). Moreover, see also de Jong (1992) and Beck (2005b), who pay special attention to Odysseus' subjective style, his character speech, in the *Apologoi*.

of which constitutes the first part of Dante's epic poem *The Divine Comedy*. Among countless other figures from the mythical and historical past, they also meet Ulysses (i.e. the Roman form of Odysseus' name) and Diomedes (another veteran from the Trojan War). Dante asks Vergil,

> 'Who is there in that fire which is so divided
> On top, that it appears to rise from the pyre
> That Eteokles was put on with his brother?'
> He [= Vergil] answered me: 'Inside there Ulysses
> And Diomedes are tortured, and go together
> In retribution as they were in fury;
> And so with their flame they now groan
> For that ruse of the horse which made the opening
> Through which came out the noble race of Romans.
> They also weep inside for the cunning which makes
> Deidameia, dead, still mourn for Achilles,
> And there they pay for the Palladium too.' (*Inferno*, Canto 26.52–63)[48]

Here, in the eighth *bolgia* ('ditch') of the Eighth Circle (the *Malebolge*, 'Evil Ditches'), we meet the counsellors of fraud: deceitful individuals are punished there for having exploited their intellectual capacities in order to lure others into fraudulent acts. Among these, Ulysses and Diomedes take pride of place, enduring punishment for the ploy of the Trojan Horse, for persuading Achilles into joining the Trojan expedition (resulting in his wife's anguish) and for the theft of the Palladium (a cult image of Athene originally in Trojan possession, described in detail in Book 2 of Vergil's *Aeneid*). Shortly thereafter, Ulysses himself begins to speak, recounting his voyage from when he and his comrades left the isle of Circe, but with an ending that deviates from that of the *Odyssey* considerably: for instead of having him return home, Dante has Ulysses embark on one final voyage, taking him beyond the Pillars of Hercules into the open sea of the Atlantic, where he ultimately is shipwrecked and drowns (26.90–142).

We do not need to examine these passages in much deeper detail to understand that Dante here revitalizes the centuries-old idea of Odysseus as the prototypical man of words.[49] Clearly, rhetorical prowess is the most stable aspect of Odysseus' characterization throughout the centuries; however,

---

[48] English translation of the Italian original by Sisson (1993), adapted to our spelling conventions.

[49] On Dante's Ulysses, see e.g. Stanford (1963: 178–181 *et passim*); Higgins (1993: 552–554); Kablitz (2005); Hall (2008: 210–213); Mallette (2021: 369–370); Lombardi (2023). It must be noted that Dante did not have direct access to Homer's *Odyssey*, and that hence Dante's reception of the Homeric hero was shaped by later (Latin) sources (see Higgins 1993: 554). There are traces of this alternative ending in Latin literature from the late Republic onward (see Kablitz 2005: 97n.5 and Lombardi 2023: 83–89).

Dante's revitalization comes with a different take, for Odysseus is now a recognizably more negative figure. This is a development that begins many centuries before Dante already and becomes a leitmotif in the post-Homeric tradition throughout the centuries, for Odysseus can be seen as an ambivalent figure as early as the *Odyssey* through his role as a liar, whereas in the *Iliad*, he uses his intellectual and rhetorical abilities solely in the interest of the Achaean community (§ 2.1). Viewed from a narratological perspective, Odysseus' role as an intradiegetic (and potentially unreliable) narrator in the *Odyssey* greatly influences his later development. Already in the *Odyssey*, Athene spells out the ambiguous nature of Odysseus' wiliness when, seeing through his lies (i.e. the first set of his Cretan lies, *Od.* 13.256–286), she half-seriously, half-jokingly scolds her protégé as 'unwearying, full of craft, insatiate of tricks' (*Od.* 13.293). And, about two hundred years later, the archaic Greek poet Pindar (c. 518–438 BCE), in his *Seventh Nemean Ode*, states that 'it seems to me that / the word of Odysseus has grown stronger than his suffering / through the sweet-singing Homer, / for upon his lies and his winged craft / there is something solemn, and his wisdom / deceives and misleads with his tales' (lines 20–23). Thus, Pindar takes up the notion of Odysseus as Homer's poetic *alter ego* and connects it to the idea of Odysseus as a liar, 'opposing the accounts of the heroic age found in epic poetry' (Maslov 2015: 124), yet at the same time ascribing a poetic superiority ('something solemn') to the art of lying.[50]

In Attic tragedy, particularly in the tragedies of Euripides (c. 480–406 BCE), we then find the notion of Odysseus using his rhetorical skills ruthlessly and almost in a literal sense going over dead bodies in order to achieve his ends.[51] In the play *Hekabe* (produced c. 424 BCE), he convinces the Achaean assembly that Polyxena, a daughter of Priam and Hekabe, ought to be sacrificed to the dead Achilles because he has asked for compensation after his tomb had been left without the proper honours. The chorus leader passes on the decision to Hekabe, referring to Odysseus as 'a crafty, wrangling, sweet-speaking pleaser of the people' (lines 131–132).[52] Hekabe reacts to this terrible news by pleading for Polyxena's life, even offering her own life for that of her daughter – but to no

---

[50] See Grandolini (1995) on the passage in further detail, and Stanford (1963: 81–117) on the post-Homeric development of the Odysseus figure in Greek literature.

[51] See Montiglio (2011: 3, 5): 'Tragedy is the main "source" for negative assessments of Odysseus and for their appeal to large audiences. . . . The great majority of them are by Euripides . . . .'

[52] On the passage, see Gregory (1999: 63–64); on the portrayal of Odysseus as a demagogue, Jouan (1984: 9–10); on the violence of rhetoric as a leitmotif in the *Hekuba*, Buxton (1982: 170–186) and Kastely (1993); on the sacrifice of Polyxena, Mangieri (2018: 62–99), with further references. Polyxena's sacrifice at the tomb of Achilles is as old as the Epic Cycle, but we do not know whether Odysseus was already involved in the corresponding decision there; he is, however, the one who kills Hekabe's grandson Astyanax (see *Iliupersis* Procl. arg. p. 89.20–23 *PEG* with the commentary by West 2013: 240).

avail; Odysseus remains adamant.[53] However, she maintains composure throughout the entire play – yet ten years later, in *The Trojan Women* (produced in 415 BCE), she completely loses composure when she is informed that she has been assigned as a slave to Odysseus (lines 283–287):

> I have been allotted to serve an abominable, treacherous man,
> a fiend of justice, a beast [that stands] beside the law,
> someone who turns everything from one side to the other
> and back from here again by his double-folded tongue,
> making disliked what had been liked before. (Eur. *Troad*. 283–287)

Hekabe uses utterly harsh words that, inter alia, qualify Odysseus as infected with ritual pollution and compare him to a wild animal.[54] Scodel (1980: 72) thus rightly sees a contradiction between Hekabe's outburst and the fact that Odysseus actually 'has done nothing to justify the particular accusations [she] makes against him' in the play so far. Later in the play, though, the messenger Talthybios informs Hekabe's daughter-in-law Andromache that the Achaean assembly has decided that her son Astyanax is to be killed (line 719) and that 'among the assembled Greeks, Odysseus won with his speech' (line 721), indicating that it was Odysseus who convinced the Achaeans that this dreadful murder ought to be committed. Thus, in a sense, we could interpret Hekabe's hateful outcry as a proleptic reaction anticipating this news. Furthermore, if we look beyond the fictional frame of the play, we may also perceive Hekabe's outburst as a metalepsis – that is, as a late response resulting from her experience with the man who condemned her daughter to death by having her sacrificed in a previous play. Finally, Hekabe's attack may also be seen as harking back to her own words in the *Iliad* when she gives free rein to her hatred for Achilles, her son's murderer, by saying 'I wish that into the midst of his liver / I could sink my teeth and eat it; then there would be retaliation / for my son' (*Il*. 24.212–214). The hatred she feels now for the man who is responsible for the killing of her daughter and her grandchild is similar to the hatred she felt back then for the murderer of her son.

Another post-Homeric incident involving Odysseus is that of the *hóplōn krísis* (ὅπλων κρίσις, 'the judgement of the arms'), a story that stages a dispute between Odysseus and the Greater Ajax about the armour of the dead Achilles, and results in Odysseus' victory and the subsequent suicide of

---

[53] See Stanford (1963: 114): 'Euripides visualizes [Odysseus] as the extreme type of chauvinistic and militaristic power-politician, correct as any Nazi Gauleiter and as impervious to personal or emotional appeals.'

[54] The adjective translated as 'abominable' is μυσαρός, a derivation from the noun μύσος, a religious term denoting ritual defilement. The noun translated as 'beast' is δάκος, 'biter' (from the verb δάκνειν, 'to bite').

Ajax. To be precise, the story must have already been part of the traditional epic inventory because Odysseus recounts it in the *Odyssey* when he meets the ghost of Ajax on the occasion of his trip to the Underworld (*Od.* 11.541–564; see also 5.309–310), and it is also attested in the Epic Cycle (i.e. a collection of fragmentarily preserved archaic Greek epics serving as prequels and sequels to the *Iliad* and the *Odyssey*).[55] However, it is first in the post-Homeric tradition that it finds its narrative heyday. The story was widely known in antiquity and treated by different Greek and Roman authors in different genres and periods, including, for example, a lost tragedy by Aeschylus (frs. 174–178 *TrGF*), Ovid's *Metamorphoses* (12.620–13.398), and another lost tragedy by the Roman dramatist Pacuvius.[56] There were different versions as to who the decisionmakers in allotting Achilles' armour to Odysseus were; however, in all cases, the decision is the result of Odysseus' rhetorical skills. The perhaps most far-reaching version is that provided by Quintus of Smyrna (third century AD), author of the *Posthomerica*, a sequel to Homer's *Iliad*, who makes Odysseus resort to a blatant lie by having him claim that he, not Ajax, rescued Achilles' corpse from the battlefield (*PH* 5.285–286) – although it is clear that Ajax, not Odysseus, did in fact salvage the dead body (*PH* 3.217–371).[57] Later in the epic, after Ajax's suicide, then, Odysseus utters a defence speech (*PH* 5.574–597) where he hypocritically feigns regret but at the same time dismisses responsibility by blaming fate for what he did, thus in fact only reinforcing his negative character.

The negative development of the Odysseus figure after Homer (beginning with Pindar and culminating in Euripides' tragedies) is often associated with the rise of the sophists in the classical era; Odysseus is thus seen as a mythical prefiguration of the sophists and the negative stereotypes associated with them.[58] There is, however, also a decidedly narratological side connected to this development. To come back to the Euripidean Odysseus, it is important to note that a major shift of focalization occurs in the passages discussed: in the Homeric *Apologoi*, it is Odysseus who talks about himself and his adventures in a long, extended direct speech; Euripides, in turn, has others talk about Odysseus and thus has him being focalized through the eyes of his enemies.

---

[55] See *Aethiopis* Procl. arg. p. 69.22–24 and *Ilias parva* Procl. arg. p. 74.3–5 *PEG* with the commentary by West (2013: 151–153, 159–162, 174–177).

[56] See Schierl (2006: 131–139) on Pacuvius, including an overview of all other literary sources. On the *hóplōn krísis* in the *Odyssey*, see Sbardella (1998) and Scafoglio (2017 *passim*).

[57] I offer a comprehensive analysis of the entire speech contest (*PH* 5.180–316) at Bär (2010).

[58] See e.g. Stanford (1963: 90–117). This development happens in parallel with a popularization of the Odysseus figure in the visual arts, on which see e.g. von den Hoff (2009). See also Montiglio (2011: 7–8, 23–24) for a slightly different take on the 'sophistic' Odysseus.

Yet, while Odysseus' self-account is to some degree unreliable, the external perspective through the eyes of his archenemies is of course equally subjective. The unreliability of Odysseus' words is conspicuously taken up again by Quintus of Smyrna, who has Odysseus resort to an upfront lie (and makes him get away with it). Furthermore, the dispute between Ajax and Odysseus structurally inverts the embassy to Achilles from *Iliad* 9 (§ 2.1): there Odysseus and Ajax were united by the same mission; now they are opponents. Moreover, while Odysseus fails with his rhetoric to convince Achilles, the best of the Achaeans, into rejoining the battle, he succeeds later in defeating Ajax, the second-best of the Achaeans.[59] As Odysseus learns from his mistake after prematurely revealing his identity to Polyphemos (§ 2.1), he similarly improves his rhetoric after the failure in Achilles' tent and turns it against his previous ally. I think it is symptomatic that (as far as we know) no ancient author ever attempted to continue Odysseus' direct narration although the *Odyssey* clearly opens up for a continuation, promising more adventures to come,[60] but instead later authors chose to shift the narrative focus away from Odysseus' own voice, signalling the transformation of his character from an unreliable self-narrator to a figure defined by the subjective perceptions and judgements of others.

3 Case Study II: Herakles

3.1 A Ubiquitous Hero without a Canon

Odysseus is without doubt the most widely travelled character in Greek mythology (and the prototypical traveller per se) – but if there is anyone who could pose a challenge to him, it would be Herakles. As we will see shortly, the most famous son of Zeus was indeed said to have travelled practically anywhere in the then known world – but he was also 'widely travelled' in a metaphorical sense: for Herakles is arguably the most famous and widespread, but also the most enigmatic and ambivalent hero in and from classical mythology. Aside from being an infamous monster-slayer and muscleman – the role for which he is known best in today's popular culture – he was also a tragic sufferer, a comic drunk and glutton,

---

[59] The idea of Achilles as the bravest of all Achaeans is commonplace in the *Iliad* (see Nagy 1979 *passim*), and it is repeatedly stated in the *Iliad* that Ajax was second right after him (implying that he should rightfully take Achilles' place after his death).

[60] Odysseus announces that he will need to leave her again in the future for the sake of more adventures (*Od.* 23.248–253), based on a prophecy by the dead Teiresias in the Underworld (*Od.* 11.119–137). However, such sequels were written only in post-ancient times, the most famous example being the Modern Greek epic *The Odyssey: A Modern Sequel* (published in 1938) by Nikos Kazantzakis (1883–1957). On the vast field of the post-ancient receptions of Odysseus' travels, see Boitani (1994 [1992]) and Hall (2008).

a virtuous Stoic, a Panhellenic national hero, a founder of cities and cults, and even (in later times) an emblem of Jesus Christ. And, as if this was not enough, he constantly oscillated between mortal and immortal perceptions, often occupying a nebulous space between demigod and full deity; he was worshipped partially as one, partially as the other, and occasionally as both simultaneously.[61] Herakles' complex and even paradoxical nature can thus be explained in various terms; however, in relation to – and interaction with – literature and narrative, a narratological analysis appears to be suited best. From a narratological point of view, what is perhaps most noteworthy about Herakles is that unlike figures such as Odysseus and Oedipus (as discussed previously), Herakles was never subject to a comparable degree of canonization. While the stories of and about Odysseus and Oedipus were 'stabilized' at an early stage through Homer's *Odyssey* and Sophocles' *Oedipus the King*, respectively – both texts having maintained the status of eternal classics for centuries until today – no canonical text of and about Herakles ever existed that would have had a similar position and corresponding influence. Admittedly, there existed fully fledged accounts of Herakles' life and deeds in the form of a few (now lost) epics from the late archaic and early classical periods,[62] but these texts never achieved classical or even canonical status. In fact, the most comprehensive accounts of the life and deeds of Herakles come from two much later sources, from Apollodorus' *Library* (2.57–180; second/first century BCE) and from Diodorus of Sicily's *Universal History* (4.8–53; first century BCE).[63] Even for the most authoritative nucleus of the Herakles Saga, the *âthlos* (i.e. the famous Twelve Labours), the first piece of evidence that unequivocally testifies to a canonical number and order of the twelve deeds comes from as late as the mid-fifth century BCE: from the metopes of the Zeus temple in Olympia (erected between c. 472 and 456 BCE). The depictions on the metopes, damaged as they are, are widely known today thanks to their reconstruction drawings from the 1890s:

---

[61] On the status of Herakles as a *hêros* (ἥρως, 'demigod') and a god proper, and cult practices combining corresponding practices of worship, see e.g. Shapiro (1983); Georgoudi (1998); Stafford (2005); Stafford (2010, with 228n.1 for further references); Larson (2007: 183–188); Stafford (2012: 171–197); Larson (2021). On the peculiarities of hero cults as compared to cults for divinities proper, see Ekroth (2007) and Ekroth (2009).

[62] Peisander of Camirus' *Heracleia*, Creophylus of Samos' *The Capture of Oechalia* and Panyassis of Halicarnassus' *Heracleia*; see also Arist. *Poet.* 1451a16–22. For the fragments from these epics, see West (2003); on Herakles in early Greek culture, Huxley (1969: 99–112); Galinsky (1972: 9–22); Tsagalis (2024a).

[63] Furthermore, Plutarch (c. CE 46–119) wrote a biography of Herakles, which is now lost.

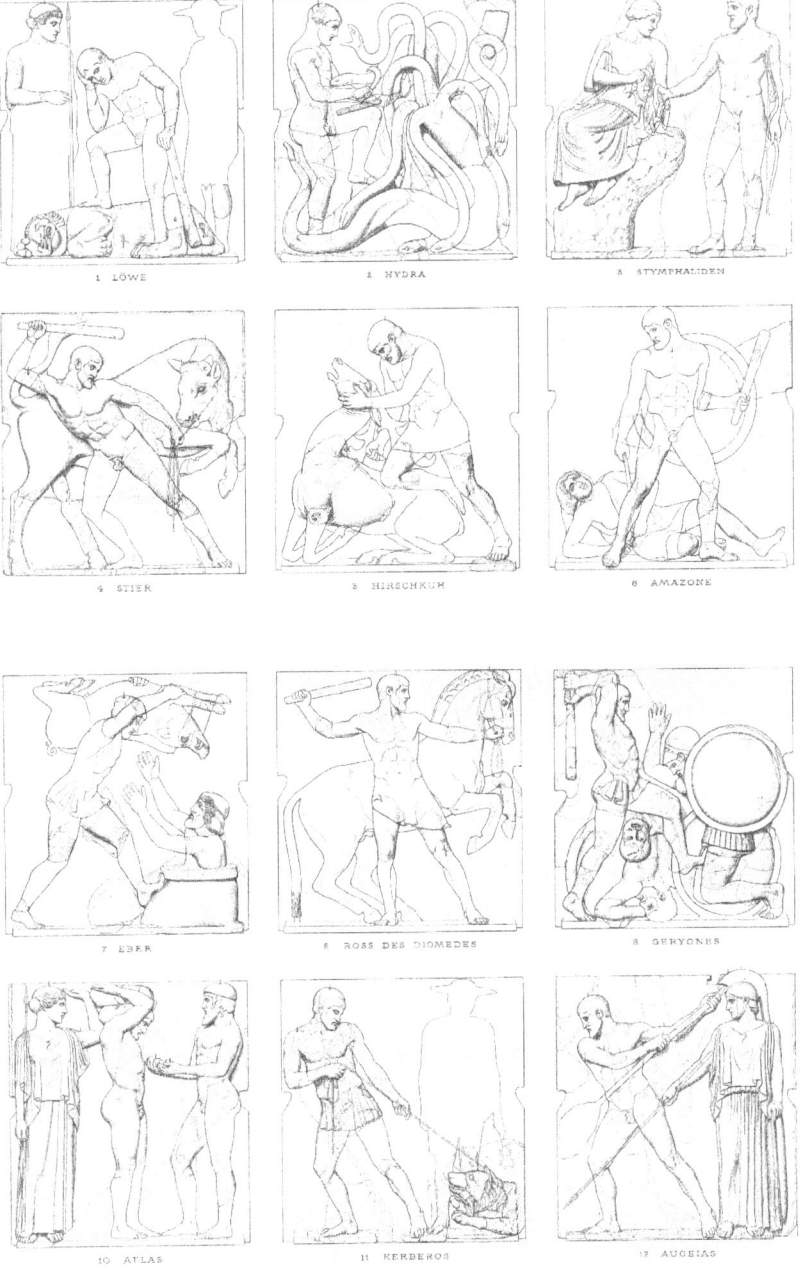

Figure 1 Reconstruction of the twelve metopes from the Zeus temple in Olympia. Drawings by Max Kühnert, from: Georg Treu (ed.), *Die Bildwerke von Olympia in Stein und Thon*, vol. 3: Ernst Curtius and Friedrich Adler (eds.), *Olympia: Die Ergebnisse der von dem Deutschen Reich veranstalteten Ausgrabung*, Berlin: Asher, 1894, table 45. Pictures taken by Silvio Bär in the University of Oslo Library, 14 March 2024. Public domain.

It is true that '[b]y the time the Olympian temple was built', Herakles' exploits 'had been a favourite subject among artists for a couple of centuries' (Ashmole 1972: 61), and clearly the metope programme on the Zeus temple must have fulfilled at least a double function, insofar as Herakles served as a figure of identification both for the athletes of the Panhellenic games, the founder of which he was considered to be (as given credit by Pindar in the *Tenth Olympian Ode*, composed in 476 BCE), and for all the visitors that came from different Greek city states in order to spectate at the Olympic games.[64] So, Herakles was indubitably a character with whom Greeks from any provenance could identify and whose name thus functioned as a Panhellenic identity marker better than that of any other mythical figure.[65] On the other hand, the fact that there is no earlier source testifying to the canonicity of the Dodekathlos must not be underestimated; the late attestation feeds back onto the lack of canonicity of the Herakles Saga in general terms (the fact that there are several allusions and passing references to Herakles already in the *Iliad* testifies to the old age of the Herakles figure and some of the stories connected to him, but there is no evidence that the Dodekathlos was already canonical at the time of Homer).[66] This absence of canonicity, in turn, holds far-reaching implications for the narrative expansiveness of the Herakles Saga, affording ample opportunity for continual variation and extension of its narratives.

Due to the hero's Panhellenic nature, Herakles was ubiquitous in ancient Greek culture – and beyond. Like Odysseus, Herakles is a traveller and an explorer, one who does not only reach but even transgresses the boundaries of the inhabited world.[67] And like Odysseus, he is one of the few humans who descends to the Underworld while alive (and returns). His *katábasis* (κατάβασις, 'descent', the technical term for a human descending to the Underworld for a specific purpose) marks Herakles as a liminal figure both in a spatial and an ontological sense: by crossing a boundary that an ordinary

---

[64] On the Herakles programme on the metopes of the Zeus temple in Olympia, see especially Ashmole (1972: 60–89); Cohen (1994); Barringer (2008: 46–50). On the canonical number and order of the deeds of the Dodekathlos, see Brommer (1953); Gantz (1993: 381–416); Stafford (2012: 24–30); Ogden (2021b: xxv–xxviii).

[65] On Herakles and the Panhellenic idea in ancient Greek culture, see Bär (2021).

[66] On Herakles in the *Iliad*, see Bär (2018: 33–44); Bär (2019: 110–114); Hsu (2021: 23–47); Barker & Christensen (2021: 291–297); see also § 3.2 below. It has further been suggested that there may be a reference to the Dodekathlos in one of Pindar's fragments (fr. 169a.43 Snell/Maehler), but the evidence stands, in my opinion, on shaky grounds (*pace* Pavese 1968: 83).

[67] On the structural differences between the two, see Molina Marín (2021: 410): 'The travels of Odysseus constitute a there-and-back-again journey; he returns to his home where his father is waiting for him. By contrast, Heracles' travels are more complex, more expansive and more comprehensive. And whereas Odysseus is a sailor, … Heracles [is] the true wandering – walking-wandering – hero.'

human is otherwise unable to cross, he makes himself worthy of his later deification. The first passage that testifies to Herakles' apotheosis is as old as the *Odyssey*; most interestingly, it comes from Odysseus' own *katábasis* as described in Book 11 (the so-called *Nekyia*): at the end of his visit to the Underworld, Odysseus encounters Herakles' *eídōlon* (εἴδωλον, 'double', 'avatar'); he is described as an intimidating archer with a quiver mirroring his nature as a warrior (lines 601–627).[68] In addition to being trapped in the Underworld, Herakles is also, simultaneously, described as residing on Mount Olympus:

> After this one [= Sisyphos] I saw the powerful Herakles –
> [that is to say,] his double: he himself rejoices among the immortal gods
> at festivities and has Hebe with the fair ankles,
> a daughter of the great Zeus and of Hera with the golden shoes. (*Od.* 11.601–604)

Since antiquity, scholars have regarded lines 602–604 as a later interpolation, arguing that Herakles' deification could not be as old as the *Odyssey* and that the two versions of his afterlife were mutually exclusive from a logical perspective.[69] However, the first argument can be mitigated by way of reference to iconography: for the deified Herakles is displayed together with his Olympian wife Hebe, the personified goddess of youth, on a Corinthian aryballos that is dated to c. 600 BCE, meaning that, at least if we are prepared to accept a dating of the *Odyssey* to the later seventeenth century BCE, there is a certain chance that the idea of a deified Herakles may not have been completely unheard of at the time of the composition of the *Odyssey*.[70] The second point, in turn, finds its counter-argument in a narratological explanation, for what takes place here is a crossover from two otherwise distinct mythical frames: an encounter between a character from the mythical plupast and the protagonist of the actual diegesis, the two characters belonging to two different worlds and different time periods both spatially and temporally. Whereas Odysseus still belongs to the realm of the living, Herakles dwells both in the Underworld and on Mount Olympus. The spatial expansion ('down' vs 'up') corresponds to the temporal dimension ('past' vs 'present'/'future'); for Herakles, time and space have, in a way, become one and the same thing. Furthermore, the fact that an 'echo' of Herakles still remains in the Underworld while his deified self abides in Heaven is an eternal reminder of his own, previous *katábasis* (which he

---

[68] See my more detailed interpretation of this passage at Bär (2018: 45–48) and Bär (2019: 114–115).
[69] See e.g. Rohde (1895: 625–627). Further references at Matijević (2015: 26–27n.2) and Alden (2017: 61n.195).
[70] See *LIMC* V.1 s.v. 'Herakles', n. 3331. On a dating of the *Odyssey* to the later seventeenth century BCE, see especially West (2012). It must be acknowledged, though, that the internal chronology of early Greek epic is still a matter of dispute.

mentions in his brief address to Odysseus [lines 623–626]) and its symbolic value relating to the overcoming of death.

However, Herakles' *katábasis* and his subsequent apotheosis and admission to Olympus constitute only the climax of an actual *tour de force* through virtually all of the then known world. And, by travelling, Herakles famously cleanses the uncivilized parts of the world from all sorts of monsters and other evils and thus extends civilization to the farthest corners, while at the same time also founding numerous cities and cults.[71] What is intriguing from a narratological perspective is the gradual expansion of Herakles' spatial circles, and thus of the setting of his doings, as seen in the geographical location of the Dodekathlos: the first six Labours are all located on the Peloponnese, whereas the other half takes the hero farther away to the periphery: first to Crete (the Cretan bull) and to Thrace (the mares of Diomedes), then to the far west (the cattle of Geryon), to the Black Sea (the girdle of the Amazon queen) and to Libya (the apples of the Hesperides), and finally down to the Underworld (the retrieval of the hellhound Kerberos).[72] This geographical expansion also enabled the narrative expansion of Herakles' achievements, for in between the twelve deeds, more and more adventures, the so-called *párerga* (πάρεργα, 'aside-deeds'), were inserted. To name just three examples, Diodorus' account features multiple such additional adventures, including major enterprises like Herakles' participation in the divine Battle against the Giants (4.15.1); Euripides' pro-satyric tragicomedy *Alkestis* (480–485/4 BCE) shows the hero on a stopover at the completion of his eighth Labour (the mares of Diomedes) rescuing Alkestis from the Underworld (an adventure which, in a manner of speaking, provides a foretaste of the last Labour, the fetching of Kerberos); and according to Apollonius of Rhodes' epic *Argonautica* (third century BCE), Herakles interrupts his fourth Labour (the Erymanthian boar) in order to join the quest for the Golden Fleece.[73] These examples demonstrate that the *párerga* were by no means minor or trivial, but of a global nature, at times even reaching cosmic dimensions – which, in turn, feeds back onto Herakles' destined deification (there was a widespread tradition in Greek mythology according to which the Olympians could win the Battle against the Giants only with the help of

---

[71] On Herakles as a traveller and civilizer, see e.g. Lacroix (1974); Ferrari Pinney & Sismondo Ridgway (1981); Jourdain-Annequin (1989 *passim*); Gómez Espelosín (2001: 54–62); Molina Marín (2021). On Herakles as a founder of cults and cities, see Larson (2007: 183–188), with further references.

[72] Gómez Espelosín (2001: 61) astutely observes that also the Peloponnesian Labours take place in liminal spaces (i.e. on the edge of civilization), like e.g. on mountains, in the woods, in marshes, etc.

[73] On the *párerga*, see the corresponding chapters in Ogden's (2021a) collected volume (part III) in more detail.

a human; the fact that they chose Herakles for this task shows his proximity to the divine world already before his apotheosis).[74] Admittedly, such in-between multiplications of a hero's life deeds were not restricted to Herakles; poets would also amplify the achievements of other heroes like Theseus, Perseus and Jason,[75] but there can be no doubt that Herakles 'beats them all' – or, as Diodorus puts it, 'as regards the magnitude of the deeds which he accomplished, it is generally agreed that he has been handed down as one who surpassed all men of whom memory from the beginning of time has brought down an account' (4.8.1).[76] Thus, to summarize, the vast geographical scope of Herakles' travels, coupled with the inherent expansiveness of his life and exploits receptive to new elements and expansions, resulted in a near-infinite narrative proliferation of the Herakles Saga.

3.2 Different 'Heraklesses' in Different Literary Genres

Herakles' narrative ubiquity is also reflected by the hero's presence in different literary genres and media: Herakles is not only a transtextual – or transmedial, or plurimedial – character, he is also highly transgeneric, manifesting himself (inter alia) in epic, tragedy, comedy, epinician, philosophical literature and political discourse.[77] I here focus on the epic and the comic Herakles, and on the crossing of the two Herakles types between these two genres. Herakles appears already in the Homeric epics, thirteen times in the *Iliad* and four times in the *Odyssey*.[78] However, he does not form part of the diegetic level of the *Iliad* and the *Odyssey* because he belongs to an earlier generation of heroes that was active before the Trojan enterprise. Instead, all references to Herakles, made either by the primary or a secondary narrator, constitute external analepses relating back to events that took place before the story time of the Homeric epics. In other words, Herakles in the Homeric epics belongs to the 'epic plupast' (Grethlein 2012: 15), that is, the recent past that is part of the epic memory of the Homeric characters – a past which, in turn, constitutes the plupast for Homer's audience. The only moment when Herakles appears in the actual diegesis of Homer's epics is in Book 11 of the

---

[74] See Gantz (1993: 445–454) for the sources.
[75] See e.g. Johnston (2018: 251–260), who aptly speaks of 'the golden mid-stages of [the heroes'] careers' that 'could be expanded indefinitely' (251).
[76] Translation by Oldfather (1935), slightly modified. The noun translated as 'magnitude', μέγεθος, can refer to quantity as well as quality.
[77] On the genre-dependent 'Heraklesses', see especially Galinsky (1972: 1–125); Stafford (2012: 79–197); Hsu (2021 *passim*); and the corresponding chapters in Ogden's (2021a) collected volume (part IV). Further references at Bär (2018: 17nn.23–26).
[78] *Il.* 2.653–670; 2.676–680; 5.381–404; 5.628–669; 8.357–369; 11.690–693; 14.242–269; 14.312–325; 15.24–30; 15.638–641; 18.114–121; 19.91–138; 20.144–148; *Od.* 8.214–225; 11.266–270; 11.601–627; 21.11–41. The following discussion is based on Bär (2018: 33–44) and Bär (2019: 110–114). See also n.66 above.

Odyssey on the occasion of Odysseus' *katábasis*, as discussed above (§ 3.1), and while the remaining Odyssean references to the hero are negligible in terms of quantity, they are quite significant in the *Iliad*. It is thus clear that Herakles was firmly anchored in the audience's horizon of knowledge about the mythical past and the world of a 'time before time'.[79] In this context, it must also be noted that the Iliadic references to Herakles are dispersed relatively regularly over the entire epic, which, as I would argue, indicates that he is meant to be evoked and remembered consistently. Moreover, in most of the cases, he is focalized through a secondary narrator who, in one way or another, uses Herakles to establish a connection to the epic plupast. For example, Dione consoles her daughter Aphrodite after Diomedes has injured her by telling her stories about how Hera and Hades once were wounded by Herakles (*Il.* 5.381–404), thus evoking a time when mortals (or at least demigods) took more liberties with the gods. Athene reminds Zeus of how she once helped Herakles during his Labours for the sake of Zeus, arguing that Zeus should now return the favour by ceasing to help the Achaeans in battle (*Il.* 8.357–369); old Nestor – the quintessentially grumpy old man – tells young Patroklos about how Herakles killed all his brothers when they were young, only to spare him alone (*Il.* 11.690–693). And, Achilles compares himself with Herakles when he attempts to console his mother Thetis by saying that 'not even the powerful Herakles escaped the doom [of death] / although he was dearest to king Zeus, the son of Kronos' (*Il.* 18.117–118). In all these (and several other) cases, Herakles serves a model function, but he is also depicted in a gloomy light, which makes him stand out as a highly ambiguous character.[80]

The early-epic Herakles is certainly more than the brutish monster-slayer and muscleman who appeals to the lower classes (the Homeric epics, especially the *Iliad*, underscore the values of the upper classes),[81] but his violent nature is nevertheless a leitmotif in the *Iliad*. This becomes evident not least through several allusions to the story complex of Laomedon: Laomedon, father of Priam, once hired Apollo and Poseidon to build a wall around the city of Troy in exchange for his immortal horses – but after the two gods had constructed the wall, Laomedon denied them payment. Angered by this deception, Poseidon sent a sea monster to plague Troy; Laomedon offered his horses to whoever would kill the monster, and Herakles took it upon himself to complete the task, but then was denied payment by Laomedon, too, and therefore he destroyed

---

[79] If we add the references to Herakles in Hesiod's epics and from the fragments of the lost Herakles epics, we have approximately thirty such references from late archaic and early classical epic; see Barker & Christensen (2021: 284–285).

[80] See Hsu (2021: 24). The negative side of Herakles' focalization is further emphasized by the repeated use of the formula-like periphrasis *biē Hērakléeíē* (βίη Ἡρακληείη, 'the force of Herakles'), which highlights the violent nature of the hero.

[81] On Herakles as a hero of the lower classes, see Effe (1980: 148).

Troy for revenge.⁸² The story is never recounted in full in the *Iliad*, but bits and pieces of it are interspersed across the epic.⁸³ These repeated allusions to a story complex that resulted in the first destruction of Troy can thus serve as prolepses to the impending second destruction of Troy – which, in turn, lies beyond the diegetic frame of the *Iliad*. In other words, the allusions to the Laomedon story complex are external analepses, yet they serve a proleptic function. Furthermore, Herakles' ambiguity comes to the fore here, too, as he serves as a helper and saviour, but at the same time also displays his aggressive nature again.

When we move from epic to comedy, we find a completely different Herakles type: instead of the violent and 'dead serious' cleanser and saviour, we are confronted with a jocular drunk and glutton who constituted a stock character in classical comedy from the fifth and fourth century. The most famous example is his appearance in the comedy *The Frogs* by Aristophanes (c. 446–c. 386 BCE), first performed in Athens in 405 BCE; at the beginning of this play, Dionysos tries to have a serious conversation with his half-brother, yet Herakles can only think of sex and food (lines 55–62). Another well-known example is Euripides' tragicomedy *Alkestis*, in which Herakles has a cameo appearance when he enters the stage drunk, thus presenting the comic version of himself, but becomes sober at once when he learns of the serious situation and consequently offers to return Alkestis from the Underworld (lines 747–802). And, from Epicharmus (c. 550–c. 460 BCE), the founder of Doric-Sicilian comedy, a fragment survives that presents Herakles as the prototypical *adēphágos* (ἀδηφάγος, 'overeater') in a completely exaggerated manner:

> If you first saw him eating, you'd die:
> his gullet roars inside, his jaw rattles;
> his grinder creaks, his canine grates;
> he hisses with his nostrils and wiggles his ears. (*Busiris* fr. 18 *PCG*)

Unfortunately, most passages that feature this type of Herakles come from authors like Phrynichos, Kratinos and Alexis, whose works only survive in fragments.⁸⁴ Therefore, it may indeed be justified to '[call] for caution in making dogmatic statements about the comic [Herakles]' (Wilkins 2021:

---

⁸² For an overview of the story complex, see Wickkiser (2021: 209–210) and Bär (2024a: 147–148), with 148n.4 for further references).
⁸³ *Il.* 5.263–272; 5.638–642; 5.648–651; 7.451–453; 14.250–251; 20.144–148; 21.441–457. The story of Laomedon's daughter Hesione, who was going to be fed to the monster in order to divert it from Troy, but was rescued by Herakles, is not mentioned or alluded to in the *Iliad*, and there is reason to assume that it was a later invention, as I argue in Bär (2024a: 153–159).
⁸⁴ For a discussion of the comic Herakles fragments, see e.g. Hošek (1963: 123–126); Galinsky (1972: 81–100); Pike (1980); Hsu (2021: 131–172); Wilkins (2000: 90–97); Wilkins (2021). Further, we know of the titles of several more Herakles comedies; see Bowie (2000: 320).

317). Nevertheless, it seems clear that on the whole, voracity, inebriation and carnal desire were the major characteristics of Herakles in comedy – or, to put it more broadly, of Herakles when placed in a comic context.

Scholars have attempted to interpret the comic Herakles as a satirical sublimation of ritual practices that involved shared meals (consisting of meat, particularly beef) in honour of the hero.[85] Optionally, his appetite could also be viewed as mirroring his role as a cleanser and saviour, as the target of his cleansing were often wild animals – which, in comedy, he would simply devour instead of killing.[86] On the other side, Hsu (2021: 131–172) reads the comic Herakles as a carnivalesque contortion of the violent hero – a contortion that would help the audience diminish their fear of Herakles' aggression. Irrespective of which explanation we wish to follow, there is always a transfer from one area to another involved. From a narratological perspective, the most fascinating aspect is the crossovers from the comic Herakles into epic. The earliest such example comes from a fragment of Panyassis of Halicarnassus (early fifth century BCE), author of an epic called *Heracleia* that focused on a renarration of the Dodekathlos in fourteen books and a total of c. 9000 hexameters.[87] This fragment (fr. 12 Matthews = fr. 19 West) shows a host (commonly identified as Eurytos of Oichalia, whose daughter Iole Herakles claimed as his wife) encouraging his guest to continue drinking:

> My guest! Come on now and drink! This is also a virtue:
> whoever of the men drinks the most wine at the banquet,
> knowing well [how to do it], and who also prompts his fellow [to drink].
> And equal is the man who is quick at the feast [to the one who is quick] in war
> striding through grievous battles, where only few
> are courageous and endure the rushing fight. (Panyassis fr. 19.1–6 West)

Due to the fragmentary state of the passage and the lack of context, many aspects of its interpretation remain unclear;[88] what is clear, though, is the crossover from comedy to epic and the surprise effect arising from it. Encouraging others to drink is a stock motif in drinking songs and symposiastic literature and can by and of itself be seen as a comic inversion of the serious battle exhortation that is at home in the epic genre. Furthermore, the cross fertilization of the two genres is spelt out

---

[85] See e.g. Burkert (1979: 96) and Larson (2021: 448–449).
[86] See e.g. Diod. Sic. 4.17.3 (translation by Oldfather 1935): 'Before his departure he was magnificently honoured by the natives, and wishing to show his gratitude to the Cretans he cleansed the island of the wild beasts which infested it. And this is the reason why in later times not a single wild animal, such as a bear, or wolf, or serpent, or any similar beast, was to be found on the island.' See also Wilkins (2000: 93).
[87] For the fragments, see Matthews (1974); West (2003); Tsagalis (2024b). For further discussions, see McLeod (1966) and Huxley (1969: 177–188).
[88] See the discussions by Matthews (1974: 76–87) and Roth (1991: 242–252).

explicitly in line 4, where 'the man who is quick at the feast' is ironically equated with the one who is 'quick in war'.[89]

Another case of such a crossover can be found in Apollonius of Rhodes' *Argonautica*, where Herakles is one of the Argonauts, but leaves the expedition early towards the end of Book 1 in search of his lover Hylas after he has been abducted by a lake nymph.[90] Several passages in the *Argonautica* show the comic side of Herakles: his first appearance is staged in a burlesque manner, as he is described arriving just in time, carrying the Erymanthian Boar on his shoulders, sweating and panting (1.122–132). This description introduces Herakles as an athletic, but intellectually limited strongman – a motif that recurs, for example, when he breaks his oar (1.1164–1171) without realizing what has happened and thus 'looking round baffled' (line 1171). Further, the motif of the gluttonous (and therefore overweight) Herakles is introduced when upon embarkment, he is (together with his buddy Ankaios) placed in the middle of the Argo to prevent the ship from sinking (1.394–400).[91] Finally, towards the end of the epic, when Herakles no longer participates in the Argonautic enterprise but is still remembered by his fellow Argonauts, the comic motif of Herakles as a drunkard is jocularly blended with the converse idea of the abstentious ('Stoic') Herakles (a motif that was prevalent in philosophical literature) when he is reported to be overdrinking on water (4.1447–1449). What is most interesting in narratological terms, though, is the way these generic crossovers are coupled with an inversion of Herakles' narrative situation as compared to the Homeric epics: in the *Iliad*, Herakles does not belong to the actual diegesis, but he is part of the epic plupast, evoked and remembered by way of external analepses; this epic plupast, in turn, provides the diegetic frame of the *Argonautica*, such that Herakles becomes a protagonist in the diegesis there. However, by having Herakles leave the diegetic frame early so that he henceforth is remembered only in the metadiegesis, Apollonios recovers the Iliadic situation to a certain degree and thus plays on the narrative technique of his major epic model, Homer.[92] We can thus state, in summary, that Apollonios makes the most of Herakles' narrative potential by exploiting his transgeneric capacities to a maximum and at the same time using and adapting the

---

[89] Barker & Christensen (2021: 288) point out that the phrase *thoós anḗr* (θοὸς ἀνήρ, 'the quick man') echoes the common epic formula of the 'swift-footed' Achilles.
[90] The following discussion is based on Bär (2018: 73–99) and Bär (2019: 116–123). The literature on Herakles in the *Argonautica* is immense; see the references in my publications and in Hunter's (2021) overview chapter.
[91] This scene seems to be alluding to a widespread alternative tradition according to which Herakles was denied access to the Argo because of his overweight; see Bär (2018: 74n.5).
[92] From a reader-response perspective, the sum of these references to Herakles can be seen as constituting a Herakles epic 'in the off' – a narrative phenomenon that I have elsewhere described as a narrative palimpsest (see Bär 2018: 92–94, 97).

characteristics of his narrative situation as found in the Homeric epics for the sake of his own intertextual games with Homer.

4 Case Study III: Helen

4.1 The Most Beautiful: Divine, but Undescribed

While Herakles is world famous for his physical strength, Helen has gone down in history for her exceptional beauty. The violent muscleman and the fair maiden do not seem to have much in common at first sight; however, it may be worth taking a second look. The Attic orator Isocrates (436–338 BCE), in his epideictic speech *Encomium of Helen* (dated to c. 370 BCE), compares Helen and Herakles as follows:

> I will take as the beginning of my discourse the beginning of her family. For although Zeus begat very many of the demigods, of this woman alone he condescended to be called father. While he was devoted most of all to the son of Alkmene and to the sons of Leda, yet his preference for Helen, as compared with Herakles, was so great that, although he conferred upon his son strength of body, which is able to overpower all others by force, yet to her he gave the gift of beauty, which by its nature brings even strength itself into subjection to it. And knowing that all distinction and renown accrue, not from a life of ease, but from wars and perilous combats, and since he wished not only to exalt their persons to the gods but also to bequeath to them glory that would be immortal, he gave his son a life of labours and love of perils, and to Helen he granted the gift of nature which drew the admiration of all beholders and which in all men inspired contention. (Isocr. 10.16–17)[93]

Not only are Helen and Herakles children of Zeus and hence half siblings, they both stand out among the numerous offspring of their father. Helen is special insofar as she is the only semi-divine daughter of Zeus – Zeus otherwise only fathered male children with immortal women, as Isocrates emphasizes. Herakles, in turn, distinguishes himself from the other sons of Zeus by his apotheosis at the end of his life. Furthermore, both Helen and Herakles represent superlatives: Helen is the most beautiful woman in the world, and Herakles excels through insuperable physical strength – so much that, as Diodorus reports, Zeus decided after his birth that he was not going to father any more demigods because none would be able to surpass Herakles (4.14.4). Isocrates suggests that physical beauty and physical strength are similar in nature because those who possess these qualities are able to exert almost uncontrollable power over others. Finally, there is another, most crucial, point, left unmentioned by Isocrates, namely that both Helen and Herakles were venerated in cult, whereby

---

[93] Translation by van Hook (1945), slightly modified.

they often oscillated between mortal and immortal perceptions.[94] Helen and her husband Menelaos were worshipped as local deities in the Menelaion in the region of Sparta, as ancient sources indicate (Hdt. 6.61 and Paus. 3.15.3), and on the isle of Rhodes, there was a cult of Helen Dendritis ('Helen of the Tree', Paus. 3.19.9–10), which suggests a role of hers as a local fertility goddess.[95] In the *Odyssey*, in turn, though she is not presented as a divinity proper, there is a clear sense that Helen is considerably more than an ordinary woman when she is shown pouring a magic potion into her guests' drinks in order to induce oblivion (*Od.* 4.219–430)[96] and when it is prophesied to Menelaos that he will be dwelling in the Elysium after his death because he was especially close to Zeus thanks to his marriage to Helen (*Od.* 4.561–570).

Since antiquity, Helen has been known and referred to as the most beautiful woman in the world. In this capacity, she is, of course, the favourite of Aphrodite, the goddess of beauty and love (exactly as wily Odysseus is the favourite of Athene, the goddess of wisdom). In a famous encounter between the two in Book 3 of the *Iliad*, Aphrodite approaches Helen in the disguise of an old woman, but Helen recognizes her nevertheless 'as she noticed the graceful neck of the goddess, / her enchanting breast and her radiant eyes' (lines 396–397). The fact that Helen recognizes Aphrodite 'through' her disguise is commensurate with an established epic trope according to which deities are never fully capable of hiding their divine nature even when they have transformed themselves into another being (human or animal); at the same time, though, it also demonstrates the emotional proximity between the goddess and her protégé. Aphrodite then urges Helen to have sex with Paris (lines 390–394), but Helen refuses to comply and instead scolds Aphrodite for being responsible for all the calamities of the war and tells her to leave her alone (lines 399–412). This, in turn, angers Aphrodite, and she warns Helen that she should not provoke her, 'lest I become angry and give up on you / and start to hate you as hotly as I've just starting loving you now' (lines 414–415). As a result, Helen is frightened and complies without further objection (lines 418–420). This

---

[94] On Herakles' status as a hero and a deity, see § 3.1 above with n.61. On Helen as a deity and/or cult heroine, see e.g. Clader (1976: 63–80); Homeyer (1977: 1–13); Backès (1984: 12–14); Larson (1995: 66–67, 79–81); Lyons (1997 *passim*); Pomeroy (2002: 114–118, 162–163); Edmunds (2007); Shapiro (2009); Blondell (2013: 43–46, 158–163); Edmunds (2016: 162–188).

[95] Inscriptions on bronze objects from the Menelaion testify to the Helen cult; see Catling & Cavanagh (1976). On the Rhodian cult of Helen, see e.g. Lindsay (1974: 214–216 *et passim*) and Edmunds (2016: 169–173).

[96] On Helen's famous drugs and her witchcraft, see e.g. Bergren (1981); Goldhill (1988: 19–24); Bergren (2008: 111–130); Blondell (2013: 78–81). Clader (1976: 32) speaks of her 'witch-like powers', and Boyd (1998) likens her to Circe, the witch who transforms Odysseus' comrades into swine, known from *Odyssey* Book 10.

passage shows that despite their common ground, the distance between the mortal woman and the immortal goddess is ultimately unbridgeable.[97]

On the other hand, in her capacity as a local deity in Sparta, Helen appears not only to have been venerated as a goddess proper, but to even have adopted the role of Aphrodite: Herodotus recounts the story of the Spartan king Demaratus (floruit c. 515–491 BCE), whose ugly mother, when she was a child, was daily brought to the shrine of Helen by her nurse; the nurse prayed to Helen that she remove the child's ugliness, until one day Helen appeared and transformed the girl, announcing that she was going to be 'the most beautiful of all women in Sparta' (Hdt. 6.61). The ability to bestow beauty onto someone is a prerogative of Aphrodite; consequently, the story suggests that Helen assumed Aphrodite's role in Sparta. At the same time, the story blends the idea of Helen equalling Aphrodite with the canonical idea of Helen as 'the most beautiful', since Demaratus' mother is made 'the most beautiful' by Helen. Another well-known anecdote that shows Helen acting like a deity proper is that of the blinding of the poet Stesichorus (c. 632–c. 556 BCE). Stesichorus was the author of a long poem that treated the entire story of Helen in a way that was, apparently, not flattering to her; consequently, she blinded him, and only after he had revoked his accusations in a corrected version (the famous 'Palinode'), his eyesight was restored (Plat. *Phaedr.* 243b and Isocr. 10.64). Almost all of Stesichorus' work is lost and it is therefore difficult to relate the anecdote to the poet's actual writings;[98] however, what is relevant for our purposes is the motif of the blinding and its implications. We may follow Blondell (2013: 117), who interprets the blinding as an 'emasculating gesture', but I do not believe that the gender aspect is predominant here. Rather, the story combines two known mythical motifs: for one, it takes up the practice of blinding as a cruel form of punishment, best known from the story of Oedipus, as discussed previously (§ 1.3). For another, it inverts a known motif that combines blinding and poetic inspiration, best known from the *Odyssey*, where it is stated of the singer Demodokos that 'the Muse loved him beyond [measure], and she gave him good as well as bad: / she deprived him of his eyesight, but gave him sweet song' (*Od.* 8.63–64). The Muse grants the art of singing to whomever she wishes; the art is granted unrequested, yet a high price must be paid for it all the same; hence the topos of the blind bard.[99] The story of Helen blinding Stesichorus for punishment

---

[97] Bowie (2019: 165–166) even sees 'a normal climate of tension between the two' at work, 'which Aphrodite claims graciously to have put aside for a moment'.

[98] See e.g. the discussions by Woodbury (1967); Sider (1989, with 423n.1 for further references); Bassi (1993); Austin (1994: 90–117); Blondell (2013: 117–122).

[99] See Bowra (1952: 420–422); Buxton (1980: 27–30); Strauss Clay (1983: 11–12).

and restoring his eyesight after he composed his apology inverts this motif and thus makes Helen an 'anti-Muse'. Even more important, though, is the sheer fact that it testifies to Helen's divine status, for while anyone can blind anyone, only a deity can restore someone's eyesight.

The reader may at this point wonder what Helen – the most beautiful woman in the world, who in parts was also venerated as a goddess, at times even took Aphrodite's place – looked like. However, our ancient texts remain silent in this respect, for Greek writers either eschew descriptions of Helen or describe her in purely stereotypical terms. In the ancient world, beauty was not something that was 'in the eye of the beholder'; rather, beauty standards were absolute, and thus the idea that once upon a time there had been a woman who objectively surpassed all others was not just a rhetorical hyperbole, but had a *Sitz im Leben* both in the world of mythology and outside. Consequently, the cultural norm does not leave room for individual beauty and hence not for lavish ekphrases of Helen's looks either – to put it bluntly, saying that she was the most beautiful was sufficient for the Greeks.[100] In iconography, Helen is frequently depicted with attributes typically associated with beauty care and grooming. This Apulian red-figure bell-krater shows her opening her cedar chest with her left hand and holding a mirror in her right hand:

Figure 2 Helen and Paris. Side A from an Apulian (Tarentum?) red-figure bell-krater by the Painter of Stockholm 1999, dated to c. 380–370 BC. Musée du Louvre, Paris. Wikipedia, public domain.

---

[100] See Blondell (2013: 51–52 *et passim*). On beauty in ancient Greece, see especially Konstan (2014); on beauty in the Homeric epics, Shakeshaft (2019).

The mirror is the most widespread emblem of female beauty in Greek vase painting.[101] Helen's beauty is, in a manner of speaking, expressed metonymically in this and similar depictions, as it is transferred from her physical appearance to the mirror which reflects her appearance. Mutatis mutandis, another form of metonymy can also be found in many texts; for example, when Helen, in Book 3 of the *Iliad*, approaches the tower where the Trojan elders sit and watch the battleground, they, upon catching a glimpse of her, start whispering to each other:

> No disgrace [can it be] that the Trojans and the well-greaved Achaeans
> suffered pains for that woman for such a long time:
> terribly like the immortal goddesses she is to look at in her face. (*Il.* 3.156–158)

The noun translated as 'disgrace' here (*némesis*, νέμεσις) is a strong term for anything that causes or deserves indignation or retribution;[102] the adverb translated as 'terribly' (*ainôs*, αἰνῶς) conveys essentially the same double meaning as its English equivalent does, expressing both admiration for and fear about the likeness between Helen and – so the passage insinuates – Aphrodite. Helen is so beautiful that a perennial war with countless casualties on both sides appears to be warranted, something that excites the Trojan elders as much as it frightens them. Feminist readings seeing Helen as a target of a 'male gaze' coupled with 'male anxieties' of course suggest themselves in relation to such a passage.[103] In addition, there is also a narratological aspect arising from the absence of any descriptions of Helen's beauty. The prevalent idea of an absolute beauty standard may explain this absence to some extent, but there is nevertheless a tension between the expectations of the readers, who are waiting for an ekphrasis of Helen's looks at some point, and the constant lack of a fulfilment of this expectation. The fact that no ancient author ever wrote an extended ekphrasis of Helen's beauty constitutes a major narrative ellipsis. Several centuries after Homer, in Euripides' *Trojan Women*, Hekabe warns

---

[101] See e.g. Lee (2017: 154–155) and Vergara Cerqueira (2018).

[102] Ironically, Helen uses the same word with reference to herself when she refuses Aphrodite's order to go to bed with Paris (*Il.* 3.410). On *némesis* as a leitmotif characterizing Helen in the *Iliad*, see Ebbott (1999).

[103] See e.g. Blondell (2009: 5–6): 'Having constructed female beauty as dangerous, and imagined an absolute standard of beauty fulfilled by a single extraordinary woman in whom such danger culminates, Greek culture devotes considerable energy to attempting to control or deny the power of its own creation. ... [Helen's] impact is conveyed not through detailed description of her body but through the reactions of the internal audience, especially the Trojan elders .... Veiled as it is, her beauty makes her both the ultimate object of desire and an emblem of the heroic enterprise as such.' See further also Austin (1994: 42–44); Worman (1997: 151–167); Blondell (2010a); Blondell (2013: 44, 48 *et passim*).

Menelaos about the dangerous effect that Helen will unavoidably have on him when he sees her again after the capture of Troy:

> Avoid looking at that [woman], lest she capture you with desire!
> For she captures men's eyes, she captures cities,
> she burns down houses – of such nature are her magic charms.
>
> (Eur. *Troad.* 891–893)

Aside from serving as an implied stage direction and from attracting the audience's attention, Hekabe's words also hark back to the Odyssean passage discussed above that shows Helen as a (divine?) figure capable of witchcraft. Along a slightly different line, I would argue that Hekabe's words can also be read metatextually: she attempts to deter Menelaos from looking at Helen as much as the theatre audience (and we, the readers of Greek literature) have been denied 'looking' at her because of the absence of any descriptions of her appearance. It is of course true that the audience in the theatre is about to actually see her – a fact that may potentially thwart my suggested interpretation – but we must not forget that the actors wore masks; hence, Helen's beauty was a matter of pure imagination, probably only symbolized by a wig suggesting long hair, a stereotypical attribute of female beauty.[104]

We noticed previously (§ 2.1) that without Odysseus' rhetorical failures, the Homeric epics would not exist, or only in a rather truncated form. The same is even truer for Helen, as she is the actual cause of the Trojan War and all its consequences and hence 'also causes its commemoration in song and story, making her a kind of Muse, associated with poetic immortality' (Blondell 2013: ix). The Homeric narrator makes this connection abundantly clear by introducing Helen into his epic as the actual weaver of his text: for Helen's first appearance in the *Iliad* – and hence her first appearance in Western literature – shows her weaving a piece of cloth that displays the battle between the Trojans and the Achaeans (*Il.* 3.125–128). This piece of cloth is, very obviously, nothing else than a reflection of the *Iliad* itself.[105] But since we are reading the *Iliad*, we do not need a lavish description of what is depicted on this piece of cloth. We may, however, feel lured into believing that a corresponding description of Helen herself might follow – only to be disappointed. Taking Helen's inspirational power into consideration, it is all the more surprising (if not in fact contradictory) that she should never have been the object of any major ekphrasis herself, either in the Homeric epics or later. There is an astonishing stability as

---

[104] See Blondell (2013: 186–187). Elsewhere in the play, reference is made to her long and beautiful hair (lines 1087 and 1224).
[105] On the passage, see e.g. Kennedy (1986) and Bergren (2008: 43–55). See further Clayton (2004) and Mueller (2010) on the metapoetics of weaving in the *Odyssey*.

far as this point is concerned – in contrast to the numerous narrative reappraisals to which Helen's story was otherwise subjected.

4.2 Narrative Reappraisals Taken to Their Extremes

Unlike in Herakles' case, the storytelling of Helen is not a matter of constant narrative proliferation and generic crossover but, rather, of perpetual rethinking and rearguing. We saw the numerous changes and detours that both Odysseus and Herakles took in their development through the centuries and across genres; however, there is probably no other transtextual character from Greek mythology that underwent such profound changes and was subject to such constant reappraisal as the proverbially 'beautiful Helen'.[106] In the *Iliad*, she is for the most part presented in a neutral, at times even positive, light – if we disregard one negative comment by Achilles, who once scorns her for 'causing one to shudder' (*Il.* 19.325).[107] However, in the post-Homeric tradition, poets, historians and orators oscillate between blaming and defending Helen, between regarding her as the (sole or major) cause of the Trojan War and excusing her from this accusation. The archaic Greek poet Alcaeus (c. 625–c. 580 BCE), in one of his poems (fr. 42 Voigt), uses her as a negative counterpoint to Achilles' mother Thetis, thus polarizing two female figures as opposing objects of praise and blame, whereas Alcaeus' contemporary Sappho (c. 630–c. 570 BCE) portrays her in a more positive light (fr. 16 Voigt).[108] In Aeschylus' tragedy *Agamemnon* (first performed in Athens in 458 BCE), the chorus scolds her as a 'ship-capturer, man-capturer, city-capturer' (lines 689–690), employing untranslatable wordplay on the name of Helen and the verbal root *hel*- (ἑλ-, 'to capture').[109] On the other hand, the most famous defence of Helen is the *Encomium of Helen* by the sophist and rhetorician Gorgias (c. 483–c. 375), composed several decades before Isocrates' encomium (§ 4.1). In this showpiece of sophistic rhetoric, Gorgias identifies four potential reasons as to why Helen may have left Menelaos and followed Paris to Troy: what happened may have been the will of the gods or fate, she may have been abducted by force, or

---

[106] Important diachronic studies on Helen include Lindsay (1974); Clader (1976); Homeyer (1977); Backès (1984); Suzuki (1989); Austin (1994); Fulkerson (2011); Gumpert (2001); Calame (2009b); Blondell (2013, with 251–258 for an annotated bibliography); Edmunds (2016); Blondell (2018).

[107] See e.g. Fulkerson (2011: 119): 'For the most part, the *Iliad* treats Helen with great sympathy even if (or because) the question of her responsibility is deferred or occluded. This may be a result of Helen's own skill, or may be Homer's way of acknowledging her responsibility while allowing her to remain relatively innocent.' On Achilles' comment, see Suzuki (1989: 20) and Ebbott (1999: 4n.3).

[108] On Helen in archaic Greek lyric, see Blondell (2010b) and Blondell (2013: 96–122, with 245–255 for further references).

[109] Hekabe takes up the same wordplay at Eur. *Troad.* 891–893 (see above § 4.1).

she may have left Menelaos willingly, either persuaded by Paris' words or overwhelmed by erotic desire for the young prince. Gorgias thereafter argues that no matter which may have been the true cause for Helen's escape, she can be excused for what she did in any case – not only if she fell victim to the will of the gods, to fate or to violence, but also if either the third or the fourth option should be the cause, because both the power of words and the power of love are so almighty that someone who falls for them cannot be blamed and should therefore be freed from disgrace.[110]

What is most astonishing to see is the fact that Helen is hardly ever given a voice in all these debates. The debate is always about her, but she never actually talks in her own defence. In a sense, her silence equals the lack of descriptions of her beauty as discussed above (§ 4.1); in plain terms, we are neither informed about what Helen really looks like nor do we ever hear her speak for her own cause. An extreme case in this respect is Aeschylus' *Agamemnon*, where Helen is not only silenced but even absent – yet she is constantly present in the wings as an unseen character, because reference to her is made on several occasions.[111] There are, however, two notable exceptions to this general silence: on one occasion in the *Iliad*, Helen blames herself heavily, in an attack of self-loathing, as an 'ill-contriving, cold bitch' (*Il.* 6.344), thus accepting responsibility for the Trojan War.[112] At the same time, this self-accusation contradicts the idea of Helen as a Muse, the role that appears to be intended for her according to her first appearance in *Il.* 3.125–128 (§ 4.1). In contrast to this flamboyant self-blame stands Helen's appearance in Euripides' *Trojan Women*: there, she blames Paris and those who reared him in a longish defence speech that amounts to a virtual invective (lines 914–944). This defence speech looks back at Gorgias' encomium, transferring the defence from a hypothetical courtroom defence to an on-stage self-defence, while simultaneously also inverting the gender roles from a male advocate to a female self-advocate.[113] At the same time, though, the speech also inverts Helen's acrimonious self-blame as we find it in Book 6 of the *Iliad*.

Furthermore, with Stesichorus' Palinode (the recantation of the previous accusations against Helen, as mentioned before, § 4.1), another, most unique,

---

[110] The literature on Gorgias' encomium is immense; see e.g. Poulakas (1983); Schiappa (1995) Blondell (2013: 164–181, with 256–257 for further references). See further Basta Donzelli (1985) for a comparison of Gorgias and Euripides, and Braun (1982) for a comparison of Gorgias and Isocrates.
[111] On Helen's role in the *Agamemnon*, see e.g. Thiel (1993: 167–197). To qualify as an unseen character, recognizable references or allusions must be made to that character in a text or a play. An instructive example is Laios in Sophocles' *Oedipus the King*.
[112] On the passage, see Graver (1995) and Blondell (2010a).
[113] See Blondell (2013: 187–188) and Blondell (2018: 123–130).

twist is introduced into the Helen myth, namely the claim that Helen never went to Troy at all, but instead spent the entire time during which the Trojan War took place in Egypt. The story is later adopted (and adapted) by Herodotus in Book 2 of the *Histories* (2.112–120) and, most prominently, by Euripides in his tragedy *Helen* (first produced in 412 BCE).[114] Classical mythology is a permeable system that is always open to variants and variations, as seen in the example of the different traditions surrounding Oedipus' destiny after his discovery (§ 1.3); and authors can consequently play on the tension between readers' expectations and potentially differing outcomes, as in the example of Agamemnon's destiny, which Homer uses to sow doubt onto the expected positive outcome of Odysseus' homecoming in the *Odyssey* (§ 1.2). However, despite all the permeability of the mythical system, such an extensive rewriting that turns everything upside down is absolutely unique; it does not only introduce a new variant of a story detail into a story complex with an otherwise stable nucleus but it jeopardizes an entire *Sagenkreis* and with it the credibility of numerous authors, including Homer. In order to preserve the narrative integrity of these texts and their tradition, the parallel story introduces the motif of Helen's *eídōlon* as a narrative 'safety net': the real Helen, so is the claim, did not follow Paris to Troy, but she sailed to Egypt and remained there for the entire duration of the Trojan War; instead, a copy of her was taken to Troy – a copy so perfect that it fooled everyone, including Paris, for ten years. Admittedly, this narrative trick ridicules the protagonists of the narrative frame of Homer's epic, but at the same time it preserves the canonical version of the story and the texts that adhere to it.[115]

The parallel story of 'Egyptian Helen' and the introduction of the *eídōlon* motif is an extreme, yet highly instructive example that demonstrates the possibilities as well as the limits inherent to the narrative potential of mythology. Euripides takes this narrative reappraisal to its extreme by staging both Helen figures, the real 'Egyptian Helen' and the forged 'Trojan Helen', and thus draws attention to the various binary oppositions that follow from this juxtaposition of the two figures that are, and at the same time are not, identical.[116] Whereas Helen is an unseen character in Aeschylus' *Agamemnon* (and elsewhere), she is seen double in

---

[114] On 'Egyptian Helen' in Herodotus' *Histories*, see e.g. Austin (1994: 118–136) and Blondell (2013: 142–163); on Euripides' *Helen*, Juffras (1993); Austin (1994: 137–203); Holmberg (1995); Karsaï (2003); Allan (2008: 18–28); Blondell (2013: 202–221); Hsu (2018).

[115] Stesichorus is the first to mention Helen's *eídōlon* (frs. 192 and 193), but the motif may be older: according to the Hellenistic poet Lycophron (*Alex.* 822), Hesiod was the first to use it (yet it does not appear in any of Hesiod's texts known to us). Further, it has been claimed that even the poet of the *Odyssey* may have been aware of it (see Smoot 2012). Gorgias also briefly alludes to the motif, but dismisses its credibility (*Hel.* 5).

[116] On the binary oppositions in Euripides' *Helen*, see especially Hsu (2018).

Euripides' *Helen*. There is probably no other mythical figure that is both staged and removed, voiced and silenced, rethought and reappraised as much as 'beautiful Helen'.

5 Final Thoughts

'The past is a foreign country; they do things differently there.' The famous opening sentence of L.P. Hartley's novel *The Go-Between* (1953) was not originally written with regard to the world of mythology, but it fits surprisingly well for this area, too, as it encapsulates many of the key aspects identified as characteristic of ancient Greek mythology, such as the idea of the mythical past as a 'time before time' – a time that is decidedly different from the present, yet still bears meaning and is vividly remembered. Simultaneously, the importance of space as a decisive factor equally important to that of time resonates beautifully with Hartley's spatial metaphor of the past as a country. Indeed, the world of Greek mythology is vast in many ways, consisting of an impenetrably complex network[117] of thousands of (divine, semi-divine, human and human-like) characters belonging to a large number of story worlds situated in different angles of the Hellenic world and beyond; of these, the Trojan Saga, the Theban Saga and the Quest of the Argonauts were the most famous and the most important in antiquity, but by no means the only ones. Furthermore, these characters and the stories adhering to them pervade almost all textual and iconographic media and are herewith transmedial, transtextual and transgeneric – or, in one word, plurimedial. While earlier research often sought to penetrate the core of the seemingly 'true' or 'original' myths, it is now better understood that the way the myths were conveyed constitutes their actual essence: how a story is told, and retold, cannot be separated from the story itself. Because of the traditionality of mythology, the principal mythical story lines were typically already known to its audience (i.e. the readers of a text, the spectators in the theatre, the viewers of an object containing a mythical scene, etc.); at the same time, since mythology is a permeable system open to variants and variations, deviations from a known version of a story were always expected, tolerated and, not least, also enjoyed (the example of 'Egyptian Helen' paralleling 'Trojan Helen' being an extreme, but instructive case in point that demonstrates how far such deviations could go). A major consequence of the traditionality and the permeability of mythology was that anyone communicating myth (an author, a painter, etc.) would in the first place need to work on the 'how' of the presentation – whereas we, looking at the picture from

---

[117] On the application of social network theory to the study of ancient religion and mythology, see Eidinow (2011); Johnston (2015b: 292–306); Johnston (2018: 121–146).

a distant past, are constantly faced with the question of how variations, adaptations and developments should be understood. Some of them may be due to differences between local traditions, some may be the result of changes in the zeitgeist; others, in turn, may be explained as consequences of their representation in different genres. Myth is narrative, but myth is not a genre – and precisely because of that, myth constitutes the lifeblood of so many genres.

It was the goal of this Element to demonstrate how a narratological approach can enrich our perspective on, and understanding of, mythology and its diachronic development. When we speak of narratology, we must of course be aware that there is no such thing as 'a narratology'; rather, there are many different 'narratologies', and the one followed here is by no means the only way of 'doing narratology' – but, I would argue, it is one that can help us to gain insight into what we would like to better understand. In order to examine the nature of diachronic narratology in Greek myth by way of example, the evolution of three iconic characters – Odysseus, Herakles and Helen – was traced through literary history. Each of these figures demonstrates how myths, far from being static, are shaped and reshaped by the narrative frameworks within which they are told and retold, and how the ever-evolving relationship between myth and genre highlights the dynamic reciprocity between narrative content and form. Odysseus, as we have seen, embodies the complexities of narrative reliability. His role as both a hero and a narrator oscillates between credibility and ambiguity, challenging the audience's expectations of truth and deceit. This duality offers fertile ground for literary exploration, as later traditions reflect increasingly negative views of his character. The figure of Odysseus thus underscores how narrative perspective can dramatically alter the portrayal of a mythic hero. Herakles, on the other hand, arguably being the most famous and most widespread, but also the most colourful and most ambivalent hero from classical mythology, is characterized by his complex and even paradoxical nature. Most notably (and in contrast to Odysseus), the example of Herakles illustrates the narrative expansiveness afforded by a lack of strict canonization. This, coupled with the hero's multifaceted nature, his role as a Panhellenic national hero *avant la lettre* and the vast geographical expansion of his travels, resulted in an immense narrative proliferation of the Herakles Saga that could be expanded almost limitlessly, as demonstrated by the example of the transgeneric crossovers from the comic Herakles into epic. Finally, Helen – a figure decidedly different from Herakles, yet at the same time sharing some non-trivial common features with her half-brother – is characterized, in narratological terms, by a constant oscillation between being staged and removed, between being given a voice and being silenced. The absence of any direct descriptions of her beauty, or of a voice of her own in the discourse surrounding her, forms a powerful narrative ellipsis that invites constant reinterpretation and reevaluation. In contrast to Herakles, Helen's myth is thus less about the ever-growing accumulation and proliferation of narrative episodes, but more about the rethinking of her role within the mythic tradition. Her silence and her partial objectification may eventually also be seen as a poignant commentary on the narrative treatment of women in myth, whereby the story of 'Egyptian Helen' and the *eídōlon* motif could be viewed as serving an emblematic function in this respect.

To finally return to a detail of the Helen Saga, it should be noted that the noun *eídōlon* denoting the corporeal 'copy' of Helen that went to Troy (while the real Helen stayed in Egypt) is also the standard term that designates the non-corporeal effigy of a deceased in the Underworld. Thus, while the illusion of 'Trojan Helen' surely was imagined to have a body (after all, she had sex with Paris), the fact that her phantasm was referred to with a word that otherwise was connected to inanimate, non-corporeal entities implies her annihilation as a figure with a will and agency of her own; at the same time, it also reinforces the question of the credibility of the canonical version of her story as narrated by Homer and others. In a sense, Helen thus also contributes to questions about narrative reliability, although she never assumes the role of a narrator proper like Odysseus. Maybe she would have had yet another, completely different, story to tell if only she had ever been given a chance to do so. Surely the world of mythology would have offered ample room for such renarration – for indeed, mythology is a foreign country; they do things differently there.

References

Albersmeier, Sabine (ed.). 2009. *Heroes: Mortals and Myths in Ancient Greece*. Baltimore: Walters Art Museum.

Alden, Maureen. 2017. *Para-Narratives in the Odyssey: Stories in the Frame*. Oxford: Oxford University Press.

Allan, William (ed.). 2008. *Euripides: Helen*. Cambridge: Cambridge University Press.

Altman, Rick. 2008. *A Theory of Narrative*. New York: Columbia University Press.

Ashmole, Bernard. 1972. *Architect and Sculptor in Classical Greece*. New York: New York University Press.

Austin, Norman. 1994. *Helen of Troy and Her Shameless Phantom*. Ithaca: Cornell University Press.

Backès, Jean-Louis. 1984. *Le mythe d'Hélène*. Clermont-Ferrand: Adosa.

de Bakker, Mathieu & Irene J.F. de Jong (eds.). 2021. *Speech in Ancient Greek Literature*. Leiden: Brill.

Bal, Mieke. 2017. *Narratology: Introduction to the Theory of Narrative*. 4th rev. ed. Toronto: University of Toronto Press.

Bär, Silvio. 2010. 'Quintus of Smyrna and the Second Sophistic'. *Harvard Studies in Classical Philology* 105: 287–316.

Bär, Silvio. 2018. *Herakles im griechischen Epos: Studien zur Narrativität und Poetizität eines Helden*. Stuttgart: Steiner.

Bär, Silvio. 2019. 'Heracles in Homer and Apollonius: Narratological Character Analysis in a Diachronic Perspective'. *Symbolae Osloenses* 93: 106–131.

Bär, Silvio. 2021. 'Herakles and the Panhellenic Idea in Ancient Greek Culture'. In Serpil Ahmetkocaoğlu, Sümeyye Kara, Umay Bahadır, Özlem Gurpınar & Özlem Ünlü (eds.), *II. International Symposium on Mythology: Proceedings Book*. Ardahan: Ardahan University, 643–656.

Bär, Silvio. 2024a. 'Heracles and Hesione in the *Iliad*'. In Tsagalis 2024a: 146–163.

Bär, Silvio. 2024b. 'The Study of Transtextual Characters in Homeric Sequels: A Methodological Manifesto'. In Diane Cuny & Arnaud Perrot (eds.), *Suites d'Homère de l'Antiquité à la Renaissance*. Turnhout: Brepols, 83–93.

Bär, Silvio. 2025. 'Zur Konzeptualisierung des Transtextualitätsbegriffs: Licht aus der Klassischen Philologie?'. *Journal of Literary Theory* 19 (2): 213–236.

Barker, Elton & Joel Christensen. 2021. 'Epic'. In Ogden 2021a: 283–300.

Baroni, Raphaël. 2007. *La tension narrative: Suspense, curiosité et surprise*. Paris: du Seuil.

Barringer, Judith M. 2008. *Art, Myth, and Ritual in Classical Greece*. Cambridge: Cambridge University Press.

Barthes, Roland. 1968. 'L'Effet de Réel'. *Communications* 11: 84–89.

Bassi, Karen. 1993. 'Helen and the Discourse of Denial in Stesichorus' Palinode'. *Arethusa* 26 (1): 51–75.

Basta Donzelli, Giuseppina. 1985. 'La colpa di Elena: Gorgia ed Euripide a confronto'. *Siculorum Gymnasium* 38: 389–409.

Beck, Deborah. 2005a. *Homeric Conversation*. Cambridge, MA: Harvard University Press.

Beck, Deborah. 2005b. 'Odysseus: Narrator, Storyteller, Poet?'. *Classical Philology* 100 (3): 213–227.

Bergren, Ann. 1981. 'Helen's "Good Drug": *Odyssey* iv, 1–305'. In Stephan Kresic (ed.), *Contemporary Literary Hermeneutics and Interpretation of Classical Texts*. Ottawa: Ottawa University Press, 201–214.

Bergren, Ann. 2008. *Weaving Truth: Essays on Language and the Female in Greek Thought*. Cambridge, MA: Harvard University Press.

Birke, Dorothee, Eva von Contzen & Karin Kukkonen. 2022. 'Chrononarratology: Modelling Historical Change for Narratology'. *Narrative* 30 (1): 26–46.

Blondell, Ruby. 2009. '"Third Cheerleader from the Left": From Homer's Helen to Helen of *Troy*'. *Classical Receptions Journal* 1 (1): 4–22.

Blondell, Ruby. 2010a. '"Bitch that I Am": Self-Blame and Self-Assertion in the *Iliad*'. *Transactions of the American Philological Association* 140: 1–32.

Blondell, Ruby. 2010b. 'Refractions of Homer's Helen in Archaic Lyric'. *American Journal of Philology* 131 (3): 349–391.

Blondell, Ruby. 2013. *Helen of Troy: Beauty, Myth, Devastation*. Oxford: Oxford University Press.

Blondell, Ruby. 2018. 'Helen and the Divine Defense: Homer, Gorgias, Euripides'. *Classical Philology* 113 (2): 113–133.

Boitani, Piero. 1994. *The Shadow of Ulysses: Figures of a Myth*. Translated by Anita Weston. Oxford: Clarendon (originally *L'ombra di Ulisse: Figure di un mito*, Bologna: Il Mulino, 1992).

Booth, Wayne C. 1983. *The Rhetoric of Fiction*. 2nd rev. ed. Chicago: University of Chicago Press.

Bowie, Angus. 2000. 'Myth and Ritual in the Rivals of Aristophanes'. In David Harvey & John Wilkins (eds.), *The Rivals of Aristophanes: Studies in Athenian Old Comedy*. London: Duckworth, 317–340.

Bowie, Angus (ed.). 2019. *Homer: Iliad. Book III*. Cambridge: Cambridge University Press.

Bowra, Cecil M. 1952. *Heroic Poetry*. London: Macmillan.

Boyd, Timothy W. 1998. 'Recognizing Helen'. *Illinois Classical Studies* 23: 1–18.

Boyer, Pascal. 2001. *Religion Explained: The Evolutionary Origins of Religious Thought.* New York: Basic.

Braun, Ludwig. 1982. 'Die schöne Helena, wie Gorgias und Isokrates sie sehen'. *Hermes* 110 (2): 158–174.

Bremmer, Jan N. 2010. 'Walter Burkert on Ancient Myth and Ritual: Some Personal Observations'. In Anton Bierl & Wolfgang Braungart (eds.), *Gewalt und Opfer: Im Dialog mit Walter Burkert.* Berlin: de Gruyter, 71–86.

Bremmer, Jan N. 2021. *Greek Religion.* 2nd rev. ed. Cambridge: Cambridge University Press.

Brommer, Frank. 1953. *Herakles: Die zwölf Taten des Helden in antiker Kunst.* Münster: Böhlau.

Burgess, Jonathan S. 2017. 'The *Apologos* of Odysseus: Tradition and conspiracy theories'. In Tsagalis & Markantonatos 2017: 95–120.

Burkert, Walter. 1979. *Structure and History in Greek Mythology and Ritual.* Berkeley: University of California Press.

Buxton, Richard. 1980. 'Blindness and Limits: Sophokles and the Logic of Myth'. *The Journal of Hellenic Studies* 100: 22–37.

Buxton, Richard. 1982. *Persuasion in Greek Tragedy: A Study of Peitho.* Cambridge: Cambridge University Press.

Cairns, Douglas. 2015. 'The First Odysseus: *Iliad, Odyssey,* and the Ideology of Kingship'. *Gaia* 18: 51–66.

Calame, Claude. 2009a. *Greek Mythology: Poetics, Pragmatics and Fiction.* Translated by Janet Lloyd. Cambridge: Cambridge University Press (originally *Poétique des mythes dans la Grèce antique*, Paris: Hachette, 2000).

Calame, Claude. 2009b. 'The Abduction of Helen and the Greek Poetic Tradition: Politics, Reinterpretations and Controversies'. In Christine Walde & Ueli Dill (eds.), *Antike Mythen: Medien, Transformationen und Konstruktionen.* Berlin: de Gruyter, 645–661.

Calame, Claude. 2011. 'Myth and Performance on the Athenian Stage: Praxithea, Erechtheus, Their Daughters, and the Etiology of Autochthony'. *Classical Philology* 106 (1): 1–19.

Campbell, Joseph. 2002. *The Inner Reaches of Outer Space: Metaphor as Myth and as Religion.* Novato: New World Library (originally New York: van der Marck, 1986).

Catling, Hector W. & Helen Cavanagh. 1976. 'Two Inscribed Bronzes from the Melenaion, Sparta'. *Kadmos* 15 (2): 145–157.

Chatman, Seymour. 1978. *Story and Discourse: Narrative Structure in Fiction and Film.* Ithaca: Cornell University Press.

Cingano, Ettore. 1992. 'The Death of Oedipus in the Epic Tradition'. *Phoenix* 46 (1): 1–11.

Clader, Linda Lee. 1976. *Helen: The Evolution from Divine to Heroic in Greek Epic Tradition*. Leiden: Brill.

Clayton, Barbara. 2004. *A Penelopean Poetics: Reweaving the Feminine in Homer's Odyssey*. Lanham: Lexington.

Cohen, Beth. 1994. 'From Bowman to Clubman: Herakles and Olympia'. *The Art Bulletin* 76 (4): 695–715.

Coleman-Norton, Paul R. 1927. 'Odysseus in the Iliad'. *The Classical Weekly* 21 (10): 73–78.

von Contzen, Eva. 2014. 'Why We Need a Medieval Narratology: A Manifesto'. *Diegesis: Interdisciplinary E-Journal for Narrative Research* 3 (2): 1–21.

von Contzen, Eva. 2018. 'Diachrone Narratologie und historische Erzählforschung: Eine Bestandsaufnahme und ein Plädoyer'. *Beiträge zur mediävistischen Erzählforschung* 1: 16–37.

von Contzen, Eva & Stefan Tilg (eds.). 2019. *Handbuch Historische Narratologie*. Berlin: Metzler.

Cook, Erwin F. 2014. 'Structure as Interpretation in the Homeric *Odyssey*'. In Douglas Cairns & Ruth Scodel (eds.), *Defining Greek Narrative*. Edinburgh: Edinburgh University Press, 75–100.

Cramer, Owen Carver. 1973. *Odysseus in the Iliad*. PhD thesis, University of Texas at Austin (unpublished).

Csapo, Eric. 2005. *Theories of Mythology*. Malden: Blackwell.

Cuddon, John A. 1991. *The Penguin Dictionary of Literary Terms and Literary History*. 3rd rev. ed. London: Penguin.

Curtius, Ernst Robert. 1953. *European Literature and the Latin Middle Ages*. Translated by Willard R. Trask. New York: Harper & Row (originally *Europäische Literatur und lateinisches Mittelalter*, Bern: Francke, 1948).

Deichgräber, Karl. 1950. 'Eleusinische Frömmigkeit und homerische Vorstellungswelt im Homerischen Demeterhymnus'. *Akademie der Wissenschaften und der Literatur: Abhandlungen der Geistes- und Sozialwissenschaftlichen Klasse* 6: 501–537.

Deliège, Robert. 2004. *Lévi-Strauss Today: An Introduction to Structural Anthropology*. Translated by Nora Scott. Oxford: Berg (originally *Introduction à l'anthropologie structurale: Lévi-Strauss aujourd'hui*, Paris: du Seuil, 2001).

Dennerlein, Katrin. 2009. *Narratologie des Raumes*. Berlin: de Gruyter.

De Temmerman, Koen & Evert van Emde Boas (eds.). 2017. *Characterization in Ancient Greek Literature*. Leiden: Brill.

Doniger, Wendy. 2009. 'Claude Lévi-Strauss's theoretical and actual approaches to myth'. In Boris Wiseman (ed.), *The Cambridge Companion to Lévi-Strauss*. Cambridge: Cambridge University Press, 196–215.

Dowden, Ken. 1992. *The Uses of Greek Mythology*. London: Routledge.

Dularidze, Tea. 2005. 'The Achaean Ambassadorial Mission to Achilles According to the *Iliad*, Book IX'. *Phasis* 5: 29–35.

Dundes, Alan (ed.). 1984a. *Sacred Narrative: Readings in the Theory of Myth*. Berkeley: University of California Press.

Dundes, Alan. 1984b. 'Introduction'. In Dundes 1984a: 1–3.

Dundes, Alan. 1997. 'Binary Opposition in Myth: The Propp/Lévi-Strauss Debate in Retrospect'. *Western Folklore* 56 (1): 39–50.

Ebbott, Mary. 1999. 'The Wrath of Helen: Self-Blame and Nemesis in the *Iliad*'. In Miriam Carlisle & Olga Levaniouk (eds.), *Nine Essays on Homer*. Lanham: Rowman & Littlefield, 3–20.

Edmunds, Lowell. 1985. *Oedipus: The Ancient Legend and Its Later Analogues*. Baltimore: Johns Hopkins University Press.

Edmunds, Lowell. 2006. *Oedipus*. London: Routledge.

Edmunds, Lowell. 2007. 'Helen's Divine Origins'. *Electronic Antiquity* 10 (2): 1–45.

Edmunds, Lowell. 2016. *Stealing Helen: The Myth of the Abducted Wife in Comparative Perspective*. Princeton: Princeton University Press

Edmunds, Lowell. 2021. *Greek Myth*. Berlin: de Gruyter.

Effe, Bernd. 1980. 'Held und Literatur: Der Funktionswandel des Herakles-Mythos in der griechischen Literatur'. *Poetica* 12: 145–166.

Eidinow, Esther. 2011. 'Networks and Narratives: A Model for Ancient Greek Religion'. *Kernos* 24: 9–38.

Ekroth, Gunnel. 2007. 'Heroes and Hero-Cults'. In Daniel Ogden (ed.), *A Companion to Greek Religion*. Malden: Blackwell, 100–114.

Ekroth, Gunnel. 2009. 'The Cult of Heroes'. In Albersmeier 2009: 120–143.

Eucken, Christoph. 1983. *Isokrates: Seine Positionen in der Auseinandersetzung mit den zeitgenössischen Philosophen*. Berlin: de Gruyter.

Ferrari Pinney, Gloria & Brunilde Sismondo Ridgway. 1981. 'Herakles at the Ends of the Earth'. *The Journal of Hellenic Studies* 101: 141–144.

Fludernik, Monika. 2003. 'The Diachronization of Narratology'. *Narrative* 11 (3): 331–348.

Fludernik, Monika. 2009. *An Introduction to Narratology*. Translated by Patricia Häusler-Greenfield & Monika Fludernik. London: Routledge (originally *Einführung in die Erzähltheorie*, Darmstadt: Wissenschaftliche Buchgesellschaft, 2006).

Fludernik, Monika. 2018. 'Response Essay: Towards a "Natural" Narratology Twenty Years After'. *Journal of Literature and the History of Ideas* 16 (2): 329–347.

Focke, Friedrich. 1943. *Die Odyssee*. Stuttgart: Kohlhammer.

Foley, Helene P. (ed.). 1994. *The Homeric Hymn to Demeter: Translation, Commentary, and Interpretive Essays*. Princeton: Princeton University Press.

Folzenlogen, Joseph D. 1965. 'Odysseus as a Minor Character in the *Ilias*'. *The Classical Bulletin* 41 (3): 33–35.

Frame, Douglas. 1978. *The Myth of Return in Early Greek Epic*. New Haven: Yale University Press.

Fraser, Robert. 1990. *The Making of the Golden Bough: The Origins and Growth of an Argument*. New York: Palgrave Macmillan.

Friedrich, Rainer. 1991. 'The Hybris of Odysseus'. *The Journal of Hellenic Studies* 111: 16–28.

Frow, John. 2014. *Character and Person*. Oxford: Oxford University Press.

Frye, Northrop. 1957. *Anatomy of Criticism: Four Essays*. Princeton: Princeton University Press.

Fulkerson, Laurel. 2011. 'Helen as Vixen, Helen as Victim: Remorse and the Opacity of Female Desire'. In Dana LaCourse Munteanu (ed.), *Emotion, Genre and Gender in Classical Antiquity*. London: Bristol Classical Press, 113–133.

Galinsky, G. Karl. 1972. *The Herakles Theme: The Adaptations of the Hero in Literature from Homer to the Twentieth Century*. Oxford: Blackwell.

Gantz, Timothy. 1993. *Early Greek Myth: A Guide to Literary and Artistic Sources*. Baltimore: Johns Hopkins University Press.

Genette, Gérard. 1980. *Narrative Discourse: An Essay in Method*. Translated by Jane E. Lewin. Ithaca: Cornell University Press (originally *Discours du récit*, Paris: du Seuil, 1972).

Genette, Gérard. 1988. *Narrative Discourse Revisited*. Ithaca: Cornell University Press (originally *Nouveau discours du récit*, Paris: du Seuil, 1983).

Gentile, John S. 2011. 'Prologue: Defining Myth: An Introduction to the Special Issue on Storytelling and Myth'. *Storytelling, Self, Society* 7 (2): 85–90.

Georgoudi, Stella. 1998. 'Héraclès dans les pratiques sacrificielles des cités'. In Corinne Bonnet, Colette Jourdian-Annequin & Vinciane Pirenne-Delforge (eds.), *Le Bestiaire d'Héraclès: IIIe Rencontre héracléenne*. Liège: Centre International d'Étude de la Religion Grecque Antique, 301–317.

Goldhill, Simon. 1988. 'Reading Differences: The *Odyssey* and Juxtaposition'. *Ramus* 17 (1): 1–31.

Gómez Espelosín, F. Javier. 2001. *El descubrimiento del mundo: Geografía y viajeros en la antigua grecia*. Madrid: Akal.

Graf, Fritz. 1993. *Greek Mythology: An Introduction*. Translated by Thomas Marier. Baltimore: Johns Hopkins University Press (originally *Griechische Mythologie: Eine Einführung*, Munich: Artemis, 1987).

Grandolini, Simonetta. 1995. 'Odisseo antimodello in Pindaro'. In Margherita Rossi Cittadini (ed.), *Presenze classiche nelle letterature occidentali: Il mito dall'età antico all'età moderna e contemporanea*. Perugia: Istituto regionale di ricerca sperimentazione e aggiornamento educativi dell'Umbria, 125–137.

Graver, Margaret. 1995. 'Dog-Helen and Homeric Insult'. *Classical Antiquity* 14 (1): 41–61.

Gregory, Justina (ed.). 1999. *Euripides: Hecuba. Introduction, Text, and Commentary*. Atlanta: Scholars Press.

Grethlein, Jonas. 2012. 'Homer and Heroic History'. In John Marincola, Lloyd Llewellyn-Jones & Calum Maciver (eds.), *Greek Notions of the Past in the Archaic and Classical Eras: History without Historians*. Edinburgh: Edinburgh University Press, 14–36.

Gumpert, Matthew. 2001. *Grafting Helen: The Abduction of the Classical Past*. Madison: University of Wisconsin Press.

Haft, Adele J. 1984. 'Odysseus, Idomeneus and Meriones: The Cretan Lies of *Odyssey* 13–19'. *The Classical Journal* 79 (4): 289–306.

Hall, Edith. 2008. *The Return of Ulysses: A Cultural History of Homer's Odyssey*. London: Tauris.

Hallet, Wolfgang & Birgit Neumann (eds.). 2009. *Raum und Bewegung in der Literatur: Die Literaturwissenschaften und der Spatial Turn*. Bielefeld: transcript.

Hamburger, Käte. 1973. *The Logic of Literature*. Translated by Marilyn J. Rose. Bloomington: Indiana University Press (originally *Die Logik der Dichtung*, 2nd rev. ed. Stuttgart: Klett, 1968).

Heinen, Sandra. 2002. 'Das Bild des Autors: Überlegungen zum Begriff des "impliziten Autors" und seines Potentials zur kulturwissenschaftlichen Beschreibung von inszenierter Autorschaft'. *Sprachkunst* 33 (2): 329–343.

von den Hoff, Ralf. 2009. 'Odysseus: An Epic Hero with a Human Face'. In *Albersmeier* 2009: 57–65.

Holmberg, Ingrid E. 1995. 'Euripides' *Helen*: Most Noble and Most Chaste'. *The American Journal of Philology* 116 (1): 19–42.

Homeyer, Helene. 1977. *Die spartanische Helena und der Trojanische Krieg: Wandlungen und Wanderungen eines Sagenkreises vom Altertum bis zur Gegenwart*. Wiesbaden: Steiner.

Honko, Lauri. 1972. 'The Problem of Defining Myth'. In Haralds Biezais (ed.), *The Myth of the State*. Stockholm: Almqvist & Wiksell, 7–19 (reprinted in Dundes 1984a: 41–52).

van Hook, Larue (ed.). 1945. *Isocrates*. Vol. 3. Cambridge, MA: Heinemann.

Hošek, Radislav. 1963. 'Herakles auf der Bühne der alten attischen Komödie'. In Ladislav Varcl & Ronald F. Willetts (eds.), *Γέρας: Studies presented to*

George Thomson on the occasion of his 60th birthday. Prague: Charles University, 119–127.

Howald, Ernst. 1937. *Der Mythos als Dichtung*. Zurich: Niehans.

Hsu, Katherine Lu. 2018. 'Distinct and Yet Alike: The Two Helens of Euripides' *Helen*'. In Louise Pratt & C. Michael Sampson (eds.), *Engaging Classical Texts in the Contemporary World: From Narratology to Reception*. Ann Arbor: University of Michigan Press, 93–112.

Hsu, Katherine Lu. 2021. *The Violent Hero: Heracles in Greek Imagination*. London: Bloomsbury.

Hühn, Peter, Jan Christoph Meister, John Pier & Wolf Schmid (eds.). 2014. *Handbook of Narratology*. 2nd rev. ed. Berlin: de Gruyter.

Hühn, Peter, John Pier & Wolf Schmid (eds.). 2023. *Handbook of Diachronic Narratology*. Berlin: de Gruyter.

Hunter, Richard. 2021. 'The Argonauts'. In Ogden 2021a: 198–208.

Huxley, George L. 1969. *Greek Epic Poetry from Eumelos to Panyassis*. London: Faber and Faber.

Iser, Wolfgang. 1974. *The Implied Reader: Patterns of Communication in Prose Fiction from Bunyan to Beckett*. Baltimore: Johns Hopkins University Press (originally *Der implizite Leser*: Kommunikationsformen des Romans von Bunyan bis Beckett, Munich: Fink, 1972).

Jahn, Manfred. 1999. 'More Aspects of Focalization: Refinements and Applications'. In John Pier (ed.), *Recent Trends in Narratological Research: Papers from the Narratology Round Table ESSE4 = GRAAT: Groupes de Recherches Anglo-Américaines de Tours* 21: 85–110.

Jannidis, Fotis. 2004. *Figur und Person: Beitrag zu einer historischen Narratologie*. Berlin: de Gruyter.

Johnston, Sarah Iles. 2015a. 'Narrating Myths: Story and Belief in Ancient Greece'. *Arethusa* 48 (2): 173–218.

Johnston, Sarah Iles. 2015b. 'The Greek Mythic Story World'. *Arethusa* 48 (3): 283–311.

Johnston, Sarah Iles. 2018. *The Story of Myth*. Cambridge, MA: Harvard University Press.

Jolles, André. 1930. *Einfache Formen: Legende, Sage, Mythe, Rätsel, Spruch, Kasus, Memorabile, Märchen, Witz*. Tübingen: Niemeyer.

de Jong, Irene J. F. 1992. 'The Subjective Style in Odysseus' Wanderings'. *The Classical Quarterly* 42 (1): 1–11.

de Jong, Irene J. F. 2001. *A Narratological Commentary on the Odyssey*. Cambridge: Cambridge University Press.

de Jong, Irene J. F. (ed.). 2012. *Space in Ancient Greek Literature*. Leiden: Brill.

de Jong, Irene J. F. 2014a. *Narratology and Classics: A Practical Guide*. Oxford: Oxford University Press.

de Jong, Irene J. F. 2014b. 'Diachronic Narratology (The Example of Ancient Greek Narrative)'. In Hühn et al. 2014: 115–122.

de Jong, Irene J. F. 2019. 'Klassische Philologie/Classics'. In von Contzen & Tilg 2019: 275–284.

de Jong, Irene J. F. & René Nünlist (eds.). 2007. *Time in Ancient Greek Literature*. Leiden: Brill.

de Jong, Irene J. F., René Nünlist & Angus M. Bowie (eds.). 2004. *Narrators, Narratees, and Narratives in Ancient Greek Literature*. Leiden: Brill.

Jouan, François. 1984. 'Euripide et la rhétorique'. *Les Études Classiques* 52: 3–13.

Jourdain-Annequin, Collette. 1989. *Héraclès aux portes du soirs: Mythes et histoire*. Paris: Les Belles Lettres.

Juffras, Diane M. 1993. 'Helen and Other Victims in Euripides' "Helen"'. *Hermes* 121 (1): 45–57.

Kablitz, Andreas. 2005. 'Dantes Odysseus'. In Martin Vöhler & Bernd Seidensticker (eds.), *Mythenkorrekturen: Zu einer paradoxalen Form der Mythenrezeption*. Berlin: de Gruyter, 93–122.

Karsaï, György. 2003. 'Le corps d'Hélène: La scène de reconnaissance dans l'*Hélène* d'Euripide, v.528–596'. *Kentron* 19 (1–2): 115–135.

Kastely, James L. 1993. 'Violence and Rhetoric in Euripides's *Hecuba*'. *Publications of the Modern Language Association of America* 108 (5): 1036–1049.

Kennedy, George A. 1986. 'Helen's Web Unraveled'. *Arethusa* 19 (1): 5–14.

Kennedy, George A. 1999. *Classical Rhetoric and Its Christian and Secular Tradition from Ancient to Modern Times*. 2nd rev. ed. Chapel Hill: University of North Carolina Press.

Kindt, Tom & Hans-Harald Müller. 1999. 'Der "implizite Autor": Zur Explikation und Verwendung eines umstrittenen Begriffs'. In Fotis Jannidis, Gerhard Lauer, Matias Martínez & Simone Winko (eds.), *Rückkehr des Autors: Zur Erneuerung eines umstrittenen Begriffs*. Tübingen: Niemeyer, 273–287.

Kirk, Geoffrey S. 1973. 'On Defining Myths'. *Phronesis* Suppl. 1: 61–69 (reprinted in Dundes 1984a: 53–61).

Kirk, Geoffrey S. 1974. *The Nature of Greek Myths*. Middlesex: Penguin.

de Kock, Elbert L. 1961. 'The Sophoklean Oidipus and Its Antecedents'. *Acta Classica* 4: 7–28.

Konstan, David. 2014. *Beauty: The Fortunes of an Ancient Greek Idea*. Oxford: Oxford University Press.

Konstantakos, Ioannis M. & Vasileios Liotsakis (eds.). 2021. *Suspense in Ancient Greek Literature*. Berlin: de Gruyter.

Kowalzig, Barbara. 2007. *Singing for the Gods: Performances of Myth and Ritual in Archaic and Classical Greece*. Oxford: Oxford University Press.

Krauskopf, Ingrid. 1974. *Der thebanische Sagenkreis und andere griechische Sagen in der etruskischen Kunst*. Mainz: von Zabern.

Lacroix, Léon. 1974. 'Héraclès, héros voyageur et civilisateur'. *Bulletin de la Classe des lettres et des sciences morales et politiques* 60: 34–60.

Laes, Christian. 2024. *Disability and Healing in Greek and Roman Myth*. Cambridge: Cambridge University Press.

Lämmert, Eberhard. 1955. *Bauformen des Erzählens*. Stuttgart: Metzler.

Larson, Jennifer. 1995. *Greek Heroine Cults*. Madison: University of Wisconsin Press.

Larson, Jennifer. 2007. *Ancient Greek Cults: A Guide*. New York: Routledge.

Larson, Jennifer. 2021. 'The Greek Cult of Herakles'. In Ogden 2021a: 447–463.

Latacz, Joachim. 1996. *Homer: His Art and His World*. Translated by James P. Holoka. Ann Arbor: University of Michigan Press (originally *Homer: Der erste Dichter des Abendlands*, Düsseldorf: Artemis & Winkler, 2nd rev. ed. 1989).

Lee, Mireille M. 2017. 'The Gendered Economics of Greek Bronze Mirrors: Reflections on Reciprocity and Feminine Agency'. *Arethusa* 50 (2): 143–168.

Lévi-Strauss, Claude. 1955. 'The Structural Study of Myth'. *The Journal of American Folklore* 68 (270): 428–444.

Lévi-Strauss, Claude. 1963. *Structural Anthropology*. Translated by Claire Jacobson and Brooke Grundfest Schoepf. New York: Basic (originally *Anthropologie structurale*, Paris: Plon, 1958).

LHN: *The Living Handbook of Narratology*. www.archiv.fdm.uni-hamburg.de/lhn/index.html. Accessed 29 September 2024.

LIMC: Lilly Kahil et al. (eds.). 1981–2009. *Lexicon Iconographicum Mythologiae Classicae*. Zurich: Artemis & Winkler.

Lindsay, Jack. 1974. *Helen of Troy: Woman and Goddess*. London: Constable.

Lohmann, Dieter. 1970. *Die Komposition der Reden in der Ilias*. Berlin: de Gruyter.

Lombardi, Elena. 2023. *Ulysses, Dante, and Other Stories*. Berlin: ICI Berlin Press.

Louden, Bruce. 1999. *The Odyssey: Structure, Narration, and Meaning*. Baltimore: Johns Hopkins University Press.

Lowe, Nick J. 2000. *The Classical Plot and the Invention of Western Narrative*. Cambridge: Cambridge University Press.

LSJ: Liddell, Henry George, Robert Scott & Sir Henry Stuart Jones. 1996. *A Greek-English Lexicon*. 9th rev. ed. Oxford: Oxford University Press.

Lyons, Deborah. 1997. *Gender and Immortality: Heroines in Ancient Greek Myth and Cult*. Princeton: Princeton University Press.

Mallette, Karla. 2021. 'The Mediterranean'. In Manuele Gragnolati, Elena Lombardi & Francesca Southerden (eds.), *The Oxford Handbook of Dante*. Oxford: Oxford University Press, 368–382.

Mangieri, Anthony F. 2018. *Virgin Sacrifice in Classical Art: Women, Agency, and the Trojan War*. New York: Routledge.

March, Jenny. 2009. *The Penguin Book of Classical Myths*. London: Penguin.

Margolin, Uri. 1995. 'Characters in Literary Narrative: Representation and Signification'. *Semiotica* 106 (3–4): 373–392.

Maronitis, Dimitris N. 2004. *Homeric Megathemes: War-Homilia-Homecoming*. Translated by David Connolly. Lanham: Lexington.

Martínez, Matías & Michael Scheffel. 2019. *Einführung in die Erzähltheorie*. 11th rev. ed. Munich: Beck.

Maslov, Boris. 2015. *Pindar and the Emergence of Literature*. Cambridge. Cambridge University Press.

Matijević, Krešimir. 2015. *Ursprung und Charakter der homerischen Jenseitsvorstellungen*. Paderborn: Schöningh.

Matthews, Victor J. (ed.). 1974. *Panyassis of Halikarnassos: Text and Commentary*. Leiden: Brill.

McLeod, Wallace. 1966. 'Studies on Panyassis: An Heroic Poet of the Fifth Century'. *Phoenix* 20 (2): 95–110.

Molina Marín, Antonio Ignacio. 2021. 'Heracles and the Mastery of Geographical Space'. In Ogden 2021a: 409–417.

Montanari, Franco. 2017. 'The Failed Embassy: Achilles in the *Iliad*'. In Tsagalis & Markantonatos 2017: 43–55.

Montiglio, Silvia. 2011. *From Villain to Hero: Odysseus in Ancient Thought*. Ann Arbor: University of Michigan Press.

Most, Glenn W. 1989. 'The Structure and Function of Odysseus' *Apologoi*'. *Transactions of the American Philological Association* 119: 15–30.

Mueller, Melissa. 2010. 'Helen's Hands: Weaving for *Kleos* in the *Odyssey*'. *Helios* 37 (1): 1–21.

Müller, Günther. 1948. 'Erzählzeit und erzählte Zeit'. In *Festschrift Paul Kluckhohn und Hermann Schneider gewidmet zu ihrem 60. Geburtstag*. Tübingen: Mohr, 195–212.

Nagy, Gregory. 1979. *The Best of the Achaeans: Concepts of the Hero in Archaic Greek Poetry*. Baltimore: Johns Hopkins University Press.

Nesselrath, Heinz-Günther. 1992. *Ungeschehenes Geschehen: 'Beinahe-Episoden' im griechischen und römischen Epos von Homer bis zur Spätantike*. Stuttgart: Teubner.

Neumann, Michael. 2013. *Die fünf Ströme des Erzählens: Eine Anthropologie der Narration*. Berlin: de Gruyter.

Nieragden, Göran. 2002. 'Focalization and Narration: Theoretical and Terminological Refinements'. *Poetics Today* 23 (4): 685–697.

Nightingale, Georg. 2016. 'Der listenreiche Odysseus: Zwischen Genialität und Normalität'. In Johannes Klopf, Manfred Gabriel & Monika Frass (eds.), *Trickster – Troll – Trug*. Salzburg: Paracelsus, 119–151.

OCD: Simon Hornblower, Antony Spawforth & Esther Eidinow (eds.). 2012. *The Oxford Classical Dictionary*. 4th rev. ed. Oxford: Oxford University Press.

OED: *Oxford English Dictionary*. Online version. www.oed.com. Accessed 29 September 2024.

Ogden, Daniel. 2021a. (ed.). *The Oxford Handbook of Heracles*. Oxford: Oxford University Press.

Ogden, Daniel. 2021b. 'Introduction'. In Ogden 2021a: xxi–xxxi.

Oldfather, Charles H. (ed.). 1935. *Diodorus of Sicily*. Vol. 2. London: Heinemann.

Olson, S. Douglas. 1990. 'The Stories of Agamemnon in Homer's *Odyssey*'. *Transactions of the American Philological Association* 120: 57–71.

Parry, Hugh. 1994. 'The *Apologos* of Odysseus: Lies, All Lies?'. *Phoenix* 48 (1): 1–20.

Pavese, Carlo. 1968. 'The New Heracles Poem of Pindar'. *Harvard Studies in Classical Philology* 72: 47–88.

Phelan, James & Peter J. Rabinowitz. 2005. *A Companion to Narrative Theory*. Malden: Blackwell.

Philipowski, Katharina. 2019. 'Figur–Mittelalter/Character–Middle Ages'. In von Contzen & Tilg 2019: 116–128.

Philippson, Paula. 1947. 'Die vorhomerische und die homerische Gestalt des Odysseus'. *Museum Helveticum* 4 (1): 8–22.

Pike, David L. 1980. 'The Comic Aspects of the Strongman-Hero in Greek Myth'. *Acta Classica* 23: 37–44.

Pomeroy, Sarah B. 2002. *Spartan Women*. Oxford: Oxford University Press.

Poulakos, John. 1983. 'Gorgias' *Encomium to Helen* and the Defense of Rhetoric'. *Rhetorica: A Journal of the History of Rhetoric* 1 (2): 1–16.

Pratt, Jonathan. 2015. 'On the Threshold of Rhetoric: Georgias' *Encomium of Helen*'. *Classical Antiquity* 34 (1): 163–182.

Pratt, Louise H. 1993. *Lying and Poetry from Homer to Pindar: Falsehood and Deception in Archaic Greek Poets*. Ann Arbor: University of Michigan Press.

Prince, Gerald. 2003. *A Dictionary of Narratology*. 2nd rev. ed. Lincoln: University of Nebraska Press.

Propp, Vladimir. 1968. *Morphology of the Folktale*. Translated by Laurence Scott. 2nd rev. ed. Austin: University of Texas Press (originally Leningrad 1928).

Pucci, Pietro. 1987. *Odysseus Polytropos: Intertextual Readings in the Odyssey and the Iliad*. Ithaca: Cornell University Press.

Rabel, Robert. 1999. 'Impersonation and Representation in the *Odyssey*'. *Classical World* 93 (2): 169–183.

Reece, Steve. 1994. 'The Cretan Odyssey: A Lie Truer Than Truth'. *The American Journal of Philology* 115 (2): 157–173.

Renger, Almut-Barbara. 2006. *Zwischen Märchen und Mythos: Die Abenteuer des Odysseus und andere Geschichten von Homer bis Walter Benjamin. Eine gattungstheoretische Studie*. Stuttgart: Metzler.

Richardson, Brian. 2010. 'Transtextual Characters'. In Jens Eder, Fotis Jannidis & Ralf Schneider (eds.), *Characters in Fictional Worlds: Understanding Imaginary Beings in Literature, Film, and Other Media*. Berlin: de Gruyter, 527–541.

Richardson, Nicholas J. (ed.). 1974. *The Homeric Hymn to Demeter*. Oxford: Clarendon.

Richardson, Scott. 1990. *The Homeric Narrator*. Nashville: Vanderbilt University Press.

Richardson, Scott. 1996. 'Truth in the Tales of the *Odyssey*'. *Mnemosyne* 49 (4): 393–402.

Rogerson, John W. 1978–79. 'Slippery Words: Myth'. *Expository Times* 90 (1): 10–14 (reprinted in Dundes 1984a: 62–71).

Rohde, Erwin. 1895. 'Nekyia'. *Rheinisches Museum für Philologie* 50 (4): 600–635.

Roth, Peter. 1991. 'Zu Panyassis F 12–14'. *Rheinisches Museum für Philologie* 134 (3–4): 238–252.

Russell, Donald A. 1981. *Criticism in Antiquity*. Berkeley: University of California Press.

Ryan, Marie-Laure. 2014. 'Space'. In Hühn et al. 2014: 796–811.

Saïd, Suzanne. 2011. *Homer and the Odyssey*. Translated by Ruth Webb. Oxford: Oxford University Press (originally *Homère et l'Odyssée*, Paris: Belin, 1998).

Sbardella, Livio. 1998. 'Il silenzio di Aiace. La revisione del mito della hoplon krisis nella Nekyia omerica'. *SemRom* 1 (1): 1–18.

Scafoglio, Giampiero. 2017. *Ajax: Un héro qui vient de loin*. Amsterdam: Hakkert.

Schiappa, Edward. 1995. 'Gorgias's *Helen* Revisited'. *Quarterly Journal of Speech* 81 (3): 310–324.

Schierl, Petra (ed.) 2006. *Die Tragödien des Pacuvius: Ein Kommentar zu den Fragmenten mit Einleitung, Text und Übersetzung*. Berlin: de Gruyter.

Schmitz, Thomas A. 1994. 'Ist die Odyssee "spannend"? Anmerkungen zur Erzähltechnik des homerischen Epos'. *Philologus* 138 (1): 3–23.

Schmitz, Thomas A. 2007. *Modern Literary Theory and Ancient Texts: An Introduction*. Translated by Thomas A. Schmitz. Malden: Blackwell (originally *Moderne Literaturtheorie und antike Texte: Eine Einführung*, Darmstadt: Wissenschaftliche Buchgesellschaft, 2002).

Scodel, Ruth. 1980. *The Trojan Trilogy of Euripides*. Göttingen: Vandenhoeck & Ruprecht.

Scodel, Ruth. 2021. 'Homeric Suspense'. In Konstantakos & Liotsakis 2021a: 55–72.

Shakeshaft, Hugo. 2019. 'The Terminology for Beauty in the *Iliad* and the *Odyssey*'. *The Classical Quarterly* 69 (1): 1–22.

Shapiro, Harvey A. 1983. 'Hêrôs Theos: The Death and Apotheosis of Herakles'. *Classical World* 77 (1): 7–18.

Shapiro, Harvey A. 2009. 'Helen: Heroine of Cult, Heroine in Art'. In Albersmeier 2009: 49–56.

Shishkoff, Serge. 1976. 'The Structure of Fairytales: Propp vs Lévi-Strauss'. *Soviet Semiotics of Culture* 1 (3): 217–276.

Sider, David. 1989. 'The Blinding of Stesichorus'. *Hermes* 117 (4): 423–431.

Sisson, Charles H. & David H. Higgins (eds.). 1993. *Dante Alighieri: The Divine Comedy*. Translated by Charles Sisson. With an Introduction and Notes by David H. Higgins. Oxford: Oxford University Press.

Smoot, Guy. 2012. 'Did the Helen of the Homeric *Odyssey* Ever Go to Troy?'. In Victor Bers, David Elmer, Douglas Frame & Leonard Muellner (eds.), *Festschrift in Honor of Gregory Nagy: Collection of Articles Written in Honor of the 70th Birthday of Gregory Nagy*. https://web.archive.org/web/20181105012352/https://chs.harvard.edu/CHS/article/display/4643. Accessed 29 September 2024.

Stafford, Emma. 2005. 'Héraklès: Encore et toujours le problème du *heros-theos*'. *Kernos* 18: 391–406.

Stafford, Emma. 2010. 'Herakles between Gods and Heroes'. In Jan N. Bremmer & Andrew Erskine (eds.), *The Gods of Ancient Greece: Identities and Transformations*. Edinburgh: Edinburgh University Press, 228–244.

Stafford, Emma. 2012. *Herakles*. London: Routledge.

Stanford, William B. 1950. 'Studies in the Characterization of Ulysses – III. The Lies of Odysseus'. *Hermathena* 75: 35–48.

Stanford, William B. 1963. *The Ulysses Theme: A Study in the Adaptability of a Traditional Hero*. 2nd rev. ed. Oxford: Basil Blackwell.

Stanzel, Franz Karl. 1984. *A Theory of Narrative*. Translated by Charlotte Goedsche. Cambridge: Cambridge University Press (originally *Theorie des Erzählens*, Göttingen: Vandenhoeck & Ruprecht, 1979).

Stevens, Anne H. 2015. *Literary Theory and Criticism: An Introduction*. Peterborough: Broadview Press.

Strauss Clay, Jenny. 1983. *The Wrath of Athena: Gods and Men in the Odyssey*. Princeton: Princeton University Press.

Suerbaum, Werner. 1968. 'Die Ich-Erzählungen des Odysseus: Überlegungen zur epischen Technik der Odyssee'. *Poetica* 2: 150–177.

Suzuki, Mihoko. 1989. *Metamorphoses of Helen: Authority, Difference, and the Epic*. Ithaca: Cornell University Press.

Thiel, Rainer. 1993. *Chor und tragische Handlung im 'Agamemnon' des Aischylos*. Stuttgart: Teubner.

Thon, Jan-Noël. 2019. 'Transmedia Characters: Theory and Analysis'. *Frontiers of Narrative Studies* 5 (2): 176–199.

Trahman, Carl R. 1952. 'Odysseus' Lies (*Odyssey*, Books 13–19)'. *Phoenix* 6 (2): 31–43.

Tsagalis, Christos (ed.). 2024a. *Heracles in Early Greek Epic*. Leiden: Brill.

Tsagalis, Christos (ed.). 2024b. *Early Greek Epic Fragments III: Epics on Herakles and Theseus: Panyassis' Herakleia and the Theseis*. Berlin: de Gruyter.

Tsagalis, Christos & Andreas Markantonatos (eds.). 2017. *The Winnowing Oar: New Perspectives in Homeric Studies. Studies in Honor of Antonios Rengakos*. Berlin: de Gruyter.

Tsanava, Rusudan. 2009. '"Cretan" Odysseus'. *Phasis* 12: 291–307.

Vergara Cerqueira, Fábio. 2018. 'Erotic Mirrors. Eroticism in the Mirror. An Iconography of Love in Ancient Greece (Fifth to Fourth Century B.C.)'. *Heródoto: Revista do Grupo de Estudos e Pesquisas sobre a Antiguidade Clássica e suas Conexões Afro-Asiáticas* 3 (1): 153–187.

Versnel, Hendrik S. 1993. *Transition and Reversal in Myth and Ritual*. Leiden: Brill.

Von Hendy, Andrew. 2001. *The Modern Construction of Myth*. Bloomington: Indiana University Press.

Walcot, Peter. 1977. 'Odysseus and the Art of Lying'. *Ancient Society* 8: 1–19.

Walsh, Thomas R. 2005. *Fighting Words and Feuding Words: Anger and the Homeric Poems*. Lanham: Lexington.

Walton, Francis R. 1952. 'Athens, Eleusis, and the Homeric Hymn to Demeter'. *The Harvard Theological Review* 45 (2): 105–114.

Warf, Barney & Santa Arias (eds.). 2009. *The Spatial Turn: Interdisciplinary Perspectives*. London: Routledge.

Weigel, Sigrid. 2002. 'Zum "topographical turn": Kartographie, Topographie und Raumkonzepte in den Kulturwissenschaften'. *KulturPoetik: Zeitschrift für kulturgeschichtliche Literaturwissenschaft* 2 (2): 151–165.

Wellek, Rene & Austin Warren. 1970. *Theory of Literature*. 3rd rev. ed. San Diego: Harvest/HBJ.

West, Martin L. (ed.). 2003. *Greek Epic Fragments from the Seventh to the Fifth Centuries BC*. Cambridge, MA: Harvard University Press.

West, Martin L. 2012. 'Towards a chronology of early Greek epic'. In Øivind Andersen & Dag T. T. Haug (eds.), *Relative Chronology in Early Greek Epic Poetry*. Cambridge: Cambridge University Press, 224–260.

West, Martin L. 2013. *The Epic Cycle: A Commentary on the Lost Troy Epics*. Oxford: Oxford University Press.

Wickkiser, Bronwen. 2021. 'Laomedon, Hesione, and the Sea-Monster'. In Ogden 2021a: 209–223.

Wilkins, John. 2000. *The Boastful Chef: The Discourse of Food in Ancient Greek Comedy*. Oxford: Oxford University Press.

Wilkins, John. 2021. 'Comedy'. In Ogden 2021a: 316–331.

Woodbury, Leonard. 1967. 'Helen and the Palinode'. *Phoenix* 21 (3): 157–176.

Worman, Nancy. 1997. 'The Body as Argument: Helen in Four Greek Texts'. *Classical Antiquity* 16: 151–203.

Zgoll, Christian. 2019. *Tractatus mythologicus: Theorie und Methodik zur Erforschung von Mythen als Grundlegung einer allgemeinen, transmedialen und komparatistischen Stoffwissenschaft*. Berlin: de Gruyter.

Zoran, Gabriel. 1984. 'Towards a Theory of Space in Narrative'. *Poetics Today* 5 (2): 309–335.

Acknowledgements

I would like to thank the series editor Professor Roger Woodard and the anonymous reviewer for their valuable feedback on earlier versions of this Element. Further thanks go to the production team at Cambridge University Press, particularly to Felinda Sharmal, for making this Element see the light of day quickly and smoothly. I dedicate this piece of writing to the students in my mythology classes, past and future, as a gesture of gratitude for their interest in, and enthusiasm for, the topic.

Cambridge Elements

Greek and Roman Mythology

Roger D. Woodard
University of Buffalo

Roger D. Woodard is the Andrew van Vranken Raymond Professor of the Classics at the University of Buffalo (The State University of New York), formerly serving on the faculties of Swarthmore College, Johns Hopkins University, and the University of Southern California. He has held fellowships and visiting appointments at, among other institutions, the Center for Hellenic Studies of Harvard University, the American Academy in Rome, the University of Oxford. He is author or editor of numerous books, including; *Aeolic and Aeolians* (2024, CUP), *Divination and Prophecy in the Ancient Greek World* (2023, CUP); *The Textualization of the Greek Alphabet* (2014, CUP); *Myth, Ritual, and the Warrior in Roman and Indo-European Antiquity* (2013, CUP); *The Cambridge Companion to Greek Mythology* (2007, CUP).

About the Series

Cambridge Elements in Greek and Roman Mythology is a series for scholars, graduate students, and advanced undergraduates. Individual Elements tackle topics that are significantly more complex and multifaceted than could be accommodated in a journal or edited volume, but they will not duplicate the handbooks/companions and other conventional resources. Rather, the Elements format will provide an opportunity for authors to explore interesting themes and newer ideas and approaches in Greek and Roman myth. Each Element will present an innovative framework or interpretative strategy with sufficiently broad implications to be adapted and further developed by readers in their own work. Some Elements take a specific theme or question and explore it across a number of mythic traditions. Others take a detailed look at a single mythic notion or figure by way of a 'case study' in a certain interpretative approach. Yet others are devoted to the interpretative history of the discipline.

Cambridge Elements

Greek and Roman Mythology

Elements in the Series

Disability and Healing in Greek and Roman Myth
Christian Laes

Diachronic Narratology in Greek Myth
Silvio Bär

A full series listing is available at: www.cambridge.org/EGRM

For EU product safety concerns, contact us at Calle de José Abascal, 56–1°,
28003 Madrid, Spain or eugpsr@cambridge.org.

www.ingramcontent.com/pod-product-compliance
Ingram Content Group UK Ltd.
Pitfield, Milton Keynes, MK11 3LW, UK
UKHW022244220326
469255UK00019B/345